entieging doesn't have to be stressful. It should be fun and fuss-free. Which is why Donna Hay has put together this collection of simple menus for truly instant entertaining. So no matter what the occasion, entertaining has just become a whole lot easier.

"If you are anything like me – almost always hungry, almost always pressed for time, in the market for a fresh idea and absolutely always put off by the daunting complexity of chefs' recipes – Donna Hay is for you ... she always saves time and never short-changes me on flavour."

R W APPLE, JR, FOOD CRITIC FOR *THE NEW YORK TIMES*

instant
entertaining

thank you

It seemed like such a great idea to turn my home kitchen into a test kitchen and the back deck of my house into a photography studio so I could stay at home with my newborn son Tom while doing this book. After all, what better way to tell if a recipe is truly instant than while juggling a baby, a three-year-old, calls from the magazine office and reviewing samples for my new home range? It took extra effort from all involved whose job descriptions included some baby- and little-boy-care from time to time. For their extra effort, I will always be truly grateful. Very big thank yous to the following amazing people: Con Poulos, so talented, so passionate, so patient. You have that rare ability of being truly creative with beautiful eye for detail. I can't imagine what my working life would be with out you. Jane Collings, the most calm, even-tempered person I have ever met – if only I could be more like you. Thanks for your contribution to testing all the recipes, your ideas, shopping trips and playtime with my children – they are hoping you'll never leave. Ann Gordon, thanks for rocking baby Kit while scanning, designing and correcting proofs. Kylie Imeson, editor, champion food tester and source of much amusement. Thanks for cleaning up my recipes and for keeping our spirits light in times of high-stress deadlines. Amelia McFarlane for the gathering of props. Thank you also to the following people: Danielle Bighetti, our nanny, for surviving the crazy house. Jana Frawley and all the staff at *donna hay magazine*. Phil Barker, Chuck Smeeton and Fiona Nillson at News Magazines. Jane Friedman, Brian Murray, Shona Martyn, Jim Demetriou, Amruta Slee, Kylie Mason and Jill Donald from HarperCollins. Thank you to our produce suppliers – Farm Fresh Foods Paddington, Fratelli Fresh and Demcos Seafood – prop suppliers – The Bay Tree, beclau, T2, bodum, Provence, Design Mode International, Michael Greene Antiques, Tiffany & Co., F Mayer Imports, VnR Australia for The Love Plates range, Georg Jensen, hwi Homewares, Magis, Royal Doulton, rhubarb, Cranfields, Waterford Wedgwood, Francalia, Mud Australia – and kitchen suppliers – Smeg and Sunbeam. Love to friends and colleagues for their moments of inspiration and support: Jo from Babybliss, Nicky, Sibella, Brooke, Chris Jones, Marion Joyce and Roger. And also thank you to my wonderful, supportive mother, father and family. Finally, a huge thank you to my partner, Bill, and sons Angus and Tom.

Ecco

An imprint of HarperCollins*Publishers*

HarperCollins*Publishers*
25 Ryde Road, Pymble, Sydney, NSW 2073, Australia
31 View Road, Glenfield, Auckland 10, New Zealand
77–85 Fulham Palace Road, London W6 8JB, United Kingdom
2 Bloor Street East, 20th Floor, Toronto, Ontario M4W1A8, Canada
10 East 53rd Street, New York, NY 10022, USA

INSTANT ENTERTAINING copyright © Donna Hay 2006
Design copyright © Donna Hay 2006
Photographs copyright © Con Poulos 2006

Cover: Parmesan Wafer Salad, see page 14.

Art direction: Ann Gordon
Editor: Kylie Imeson
Food editor: Jane Collings

Reproduction by Graphic Print Group, Adelaide, Australia.
Produced in Hong Kong by Phoenix Offset on 157gsm Chinese Matt Art.

Library of Congress Cataloguing-and-Publication data is available on request.

ISBN 0061236268
ISBN 9780061236266

First ECCO edition 2006
06 07 08 09 16 /IMP 10 9 8 7 6 5 4 3 2 1

instant entertaining

donna hay

photography by con poulos

contents

introduction

One of my favourite things to do is sit around the table with family and friends, watching them enjoy great food, wine and conversation. It's what memories are made of. But we all lead busy lives and sometimes the thought of cooking for twelve, six or even two can be a little daunting. So that's why I've put together this collection of simple but special recipes that will make your lunch, dinner party or barbecue a memorable occasion for all the right reasons. With this book, entertaining is no longer stressful, it's a pleasure. Each menu, including starter, main, side and dessert, is clearly presented so you can choose which one suits. And it's not just the food, each chapter has simple style ideas that can be done in seconds – the perfect finishing touch for your table. So pick a menu, invite your guests and have fun entertaining.

weeknights

weeknights
Having people over for dinner during the week doesn't have to be a big production. With just a little effort, you'll have an impressive dinner to serve in no time. So invite your friends this week, life's too short to only entertain on the weekends.

EASY ITALIAN
starter   parmesan wafer salad
main   veal with olives and pine nuts
side   crispy roast potatoes
dessert   roasted peach bruschetta

ASIAN FEAST
starter   sesame salt sugar snap peas
main   wok-fried salt and pepper chicken
side   peanut and coriander noodles
dessert   coconut and lime ice-cream sandwiches

BISTRO BASICS
starter   asparagus with simple lemon hollandaise
main   garlic butter steaks
dessert   molten chocolate cakes

LAST-MINUTE DINNER
starter   haloumi in vine leaves
main   chilli, garlic and lemon chicken
dessert   ice-cream tiramisu

GREEK INSPIRED
starter   seared fetta salad
main   oregano roast lamb
side   dill potatoes
dessert   lemon yoghurt panna cotta

SUMMER NIGHT
starter   peaches wrapped in prosciutto
main   lemon, ricotta and pea pasta
dessert   strawberry shortcakes

EASY ITALIAN

starter
parmesan wafer salad

main
veal with olives and pine nuts

side
crispy roast potatoes

dessert
roasted peach bruschetta

parmesan wafer salad

veal with olives and pine nuts + crispy roast potatoes

parmesan wafer salad

1 cup grated parmesan cheese
2 red apples, thinly sliced
80g (3 oz) rocket (arugula) leaves
1½ tablespoons balsamic vinegar*
1 tablespoon olive oil
sea salt and cracked black pepper
150g (5 oz) goat's cheese

Preheat the oven to 180°C (355°F). Arrange 8 x 1½ tablespoons of parmesan in circles on a baking tray lined with non-stick baking paper and bake for 10 minutes or until crispy. Set aside to cool. Toss the apple and rocket in the combined vinegar, oil, salt and pepper. Arrange on serving plates with the goat's cheese and parmesan wafers. Serves 4.

veal with olives and pine nuts

⅔ cup pine nuts, toasted
8 black olives, pitted and chopped
1 cup flat-leaf parsley leaves
2 tablespoons lemon juice
sea salt and cracked black pepper
plain (all-purpose) flour for dusting
8 x 100g (3½ oz) veal schnitzel steaks
80g (3 oz) butter

Combine the pine nuts, olives, parsley, lemon juice, salt and pepper and set aside. Place the flour in a shallow dish. Press the veal into the flour to coat and shake off excess. Place the butter in a frying pan over high heat and melt. Add half the veal and cook for 1 minute each side or until cooked to your liking. Repeat with the remaining veal. Place the veal on serving plates, top with the pine nut mixture and drizzle with the pan juices. Serve with the crispy roast potatoes. Serves 4.

crispy roast potatoes

190g (6½ oz) roasting potatoes*, peeled and chopped
¼ cup (2 fl oz) olive oil
1 tablespoon rosemary leaves
1 tablespoon sage leaves
sea salt

Preheat the oven to 200°C (390°F). Pat the potatoes dry with a tea towel, place in a baking dish lined with non-stick baking paper and toss with the oil, rosemary, sage and salt. Roast for 45–50 minutes or until cooked through and golden. Serve with the veal with olives and pine nuts. Serves 4.

roasted peach bruschetta

4 slices wood-fired or crusty bread
soft butter for spreading
¼ cup caster (superfine) sugar
2–3 peaches, stones removed and thickly sliced

Preheat the oven to 200°C (390°F). Spread both sides of the bread with the butter and place on a baking tray lined with non-stick baking paper. Sprinkle each slice with half the sugar and top generously with the peach. Sprinkle with the remaining sugar and bake for 20 minutes or until the bread is crisp and the peaches are lightly golden. Serve with thick (double) cream or vanilla bean ice-cream. Serves 4.

roasted peach bruschetta

ASIAN FEAST

starter
sesame salt sugar snap peas

main
wok-fried salt and pepper chicken

side
peanut and coriander noodles

dessert
coconut and lime ice-cream sandwiches

sesame salt sugar snap peas

wok-fried salt and pepper chicken + peanut and coriander noodles

sesame salt sugar snap peas

500g (1 lb) sugar snap peas, trimmed
2 teaspoons sesame oil
¼ cup (2 fl oz) lemon juice
1 tablespoon sesame seeds, toasted
sea salt

Steam the sugar snap peas over boiling water for 1–2 minutes
or until tender and bright green. Toss with the sesame oil,
lemon juice, sesame seeds and salt and serve warm as a
snack with drinks. Serves 4.

wok-fried salt and pepper chicken

1 tablespoon flaked sea salt
2 teaspoons finely cracked szechwan* or black peppercorns
2 large mild red chillies, seeded and chopped
1 teaspoon chinese five-spice powder*
4 chicken breast fillets, trimmed and quartered
1 tablespoon vegetable oil
400g (14 oz) broccolini*, trimmed and halved

Combine the salt, szechwan pepper, chilli and five-spice
powder in a bowl. Toss the chicken in the spice mixture to
coat. Heat half the oil in a wok or large frying pan over high
heat. Add the half the chicken and cook, stirring occasionally,
for 7 minutes or until cooked through. Remove from the pan
and keep warm. Repeat with the remaining oil and chicken.
Add the broccolini to the pan for the last 4–5 minutes. To
serve, place the chicken and broccolini on a serving plate
with the peanut and coriander noodles. Serves 4.

peanut and coriander noodles

375g (13 oz) dry rice noodles
2 tablespoons vegetable oil
1 cup chopped unsalted roasted peanuts
2 large red chillies, seeded and chopped
1 tablespoon grated ginger
6 green onions (scallions), sliced
1½ tablespoons fish sauce*
2 tablespoons lime juice
1 cup mint leaves
1 cup coriander (cilantro) leaves

Soak the noodles in boiling water for 5 minutes. Drain. Heat
the oil in a frying pan or wok over high heat. Add the peanuts,
chilli and ginger and cook for 2–3 minutes or until the peanuts
are golden. Toss the peanut mixture with the noodles, green
onions, fish sauce, lime juice, mint and coriander. Serve with
the wok-fried salt and pepper chicken. Serves 4.

coconut and lime ice-cream sandwiches

4 scoops vanilla bean ice-cream
8 thin store-bought sweet biscuits or vanilla snap biscuits*
1 cup flaked coconut, toasted
1 tablespoon finely grated lime rind

Place the ice-cream on half of the biscuits. Combine the
coconut and lime rind and sprinkle some of it on top of the
ice-cream. Place the remaining coconut mixture on a flat plate.
Top the ice-cream with the remaining biscuits and roll the
sides in the coconut mixture. Serve immediately. Serves 4.

coconut and lime ice-cream sandwiches

BISTRO BASICS

starter

asparagus with simple
lemon hollandaise

main

garlic butter steaks

dessert

molten chocolate cakes

asparagus with simple lemon hollandaise

garlic butter steaks

asparagus with simple lemon hollandaise

500g (1 lb) asparagus, trimmed
rocket (arugula) to serve
cracked black pepper
simple lemon hollandaise
125g (4 oz) butter
1 tablespoon lemon juice
3 egg yolks
sea salt

Steam the asparagus until just tender, set aside and keep warm. To make the simple lemon hollandaise, place the butter and lemon juice in a saucepan over low–medium heat until bubbling. Place the egg yolks in a blender and with the motor running on high, slowly add the hot butter mixture and continue to blend until thick. Stir though the salt. To serve, place the asparagus on serving plates, spoon over the simple lemon hollandaise and serve with the rocket and pepper. Serves 4.

garlic butter steaks

80g (3 oz) butter
2 tablespoons olive oil
2 teaspoons dijon mustard
1 clove garlic, crushed
sea salt and cracked black pepper
4 flat (field) mushrooms
8 x 75g (3 oz) thin boneless sirloin or fillet steaks, fat removed
2 cups baby spinach leaves, wilted

Combine the butter, oil, mustard, garlic, salt and pepper in a bowl. Heat a large frying pan over high heat. Brush the mushrooms with the butter mixture and cook for 2 minutes each side or until cooked. Remove from the pan and keep warm. Brush the steaks with the butter mixture and cook for 2 minutes each side or until cooked to your liking. Remove from the pan and keep warm. Add the remaining butter mixture to the pan and heat for 30 seconds or until warm. Place the spinach on serving plates and top with the steaks and mushrooms and pour over the butter mixture. Serves 4.

molten chocolate cakes

¼ cup plain (all-purpose) flour, sifted
⅓ cup icing (confectioner's) sugar, sifted
¾ cup almond meal* (ground almonds)
2 egg whites, beaten
80g (3 oz) butter, melted
160g (6 oz) dark chocolate, melted
4 x 10g (⅓ oz) squares dark chocolate
raspberries to serve

Preheat the oven to 150°C (300°F). Place the flour, sugar, almond meal, egg whites, butter and chocolate in a bowl and mix well to combine. Spoon half the mixture into 4 x ½ cup (4 fl oz) capacity lightly greased ovenproof dishes. Place the chocolate squares on top of the mixture and top with remaining the mixture. Bake for 20 minutes or until cooked but gooey in the middle. Stand in the dish for 5 minutes before turning out. Serve with the raspberries. Serves 4.

An impressive dessert that is easy and quick to make – that's exactly what the molten chocolate cakes are. The chocolate centre stays soft for around an hour after baking. The cakes can still be made ahead of time, simply put them in the microwave for a few seconds on medium–high or place them on serving plates in a 150°C (300°F) oven for a few minutes to soften the centres again.

molten chocolate cakes

LAST-MINUTE DINNER

starter

haloumi in vine leaves

main

chilli, garlic and lemon chicken

dessert

ice-cream tiramisu

haloumi in vine leaves

chilli, garlic and lemon chicken

haloumi in vine leaves

4 large vine leaves* in brine, rinsed and dried
olive oil for brushing
250g (8 oz) haloumi cheese*, sliced into four
2 tablespoons oregano leaves
2 tablespoons finely grated lemon rind
cracked black pepper
2 oxheart (beef steak) tomatoes*, sliced
rocket (arugula) leaves to serve

Preheat the oven to 180°C (355°F). Brush the leaves with the oil. Place a slice of haloumi on each leaf, sprinkle with the oregano, lemon rind and pepper. Fold the leaf around the haloumi to enclose. Place on a baking tray lined with non-stick baking paper and bake for 10 minutes or until the haloumi is melted. Serve warm with the tomatoes and rocket. Serves 4.

chilli, garlic and lemon chicken

1 tablespoon olive oil
1 tablespoon sage leaves
2 tablespoons salted capers*, rinsed and dried
2 cloves garlic, sliced
1 large mild red chilli, chopped
1 tablespoon shredded lemon rind
1 tablespoon olive oil, extra
4 chicken breast fillets, cut into thirds
steamed green beans to serve
lemon wedges to serve

Heat the oil in a frying pan over medium–high heat. Add the sage, capers, garlic, chilli and lemon rind and cook for 2 minutes or until fragrant. Remove from the pan and set aside. Heat the extra oil in the pan. Add the chicken and cook for 3–4 minutes each side or until cooked through. Place on serving plates and top with the caper mixture. Serve with the green beans and lemon wedges. Serves 4.

ice-cream tiramisu

2 tablespoons espresso coffee
¼ cup (2 fl oz) coffee liqueur
8 small store-bought sponge finger (savoiardi) biscuits*
4 large scoops vanilla bean ice-cream
chocolate flakes to serve

Combine the espresso and liqueur. Place two biscuits on each serving plate, spoon over some of the espresso mixture and top with the ice-cream. Spoon over the remaining espresso mixture, sprinkle with the chocolate flakes and serve. Serves 4.

This is the ideal last-minute dinner menu as many of the ingredients can be swapped for whatever is in the fridge and pantry or available at the corner store. Use fetta or goat's cheese instead of the haloumi, and swap the chicken for firm white fish fillets*. For the dessert, use any flavour ice-cream available. If there's no coffee liqueur in the liquor cabinet, add a little sugar to the espresso instead.

ice-cream tiramisu

GREEK INSPIRED

starter

seared fetta salad

main

oregano roast lamb

side

dill potatoes

dessert

lemon yoghurt panna cotta

seared fetta salad

oregano roast lamb + dill potatoes

seared fetta salad

250g (8 oz) firm fetta cheese, quartered
olive oil for brushing
2 cucumbers, seeded and chopped lengthwise
2 tomatoes*, thickly sliced
½ cup chopped flat-leaf parsley leaves
cracked black pepper
olive oil, extra, for drizzling
lemon wedges to serve

Heat a non-stick frying pan over high heat. Pat the fetta dry with absorbent paper, brush with the oil and place in the pan. Cook for 1 minute each side or until golden. To serve, arrange the cucumbers, tomato and parsley on serving plates. Top with the fetta, sprinkle with the pepper and drizzle with the extra oil. Serve with the lemon. Serves 4.

oregano roast lamb

650g (21 oz) boneless lamb backstrap, trimmed
sea salt and cracked black pepper
1 bunch oregano
olive oil to drizzle
¼ cup honey
¼ cup dijon mustard

Preheat the oven to 200°C (390°F). Rub the lamb with the salt and pepper. Separate the oregano into small sprigs and tie to the lamb with kitchen string. Place on a baking tray lined with non-stick baking paper and drizzle with the oil. Roast for 10 minutes or until cooked to your liking. Mix the honey and mustard and place in a small serving bowl. Serve with the lamb and the dill potatoes. Serves 4.

dill potatoes

850g (28 oz) kipfler (fingerling) potatoes, sliced,
    cooked and cooled
½ red onion, finely sliced
¼ cup roughly chopped dill
½ cup flat-leaf parsley leaves
3 tablespoons white wine vinegar*
1 tablespoon sugar
2 tablespoons fruity olive oil
1 tablespoon dijon mustard
sea salt and cracked black pepper

Place the potato, onion, dill and parsley in a serving bowl and toss to combine. Whisk together the vinegar, sugar, oil, mustard, salt and pepper and pour over the salad and toss to combine. Serve immediately with the oregano roast lamb. Serves 4.

lemon yoghurt panna cotta

1 cup (8 fl oz) (single or pouring) cream*
½ cup (4 fl oz) milk
2 teaspoons powdered gelatine
2 tablespoons water
½ cup icing (confectioner's) sugar, sifted
1 teaspoon finely grated lemon rind
2 tablespoons lemon juice
¾ cup thick natural yoghurt
blueberries to serve

Place the cream and milk in small saucepan over low–medium heat and simmer for 5–6 minutes. Combine the gelatine and water and set aside for 5 minutes. Remove the cream mixture from the heat, add the icing sugar and stir until dissolved. Add the gelatine mixture, lemon rind and lemon juice and stir until combined. Whisk in the yoghurt. Pour into 4 x ½ cup (4 fl oz) capacity cups and refrigerate for 4 hours or until firm. Serve with the blueberries. Serves 4.

lemon yoghurt panna cotta

SUMMER NIGHT

starter

peaches wrapped in prosciutto

main

lemon, ricotta and pea pasta

dessert

strawberry shortcakes

peaches wrapped in prosciutto

lemon, ricotta and pea pasta

peaches wrapped in prosciutto

2 peaches
6 slices prosciutto*, halved
80g (3 oz) rocket (arugula) or mixed lettuce or salad leaves
½ cup (4 fl oz) balsamic vinegar*
¼ cup brown sugar
cracked black pepper

Cut each peach into six wedges and wrap in the prosciutto. Place on serving plates with the rocket. Place the vinegar and sugar into a non-stick frying pan over high heat and boil until thickened. Cool slightly, spoon over the peaches, sprinkle with the pepper and serve. Serves 4.

lemon, ricotta and pea pasta

400g (14 oz) pappardelle or wide ribbon pasta
¼ cup (2 fl oz) lemon juice
3 tablespoons olive oil
1 cup cooked green peas
½ cup sliced mint leaves
sea salt and cracked black pepper
500g (1 lb) fresh ricotta cheese
grated parmesan cheese to serve

Place the pasta in a large saucepan of salted boiling water and cook for 10–12 minutes or until al dente. Drain and return to the pan. Toss the pasta with the lemon juice, oil, peas, mint, salt and pepper. Add the ricotta and mix gently. Spoon onto serving plates and top with the parmesan. Serves 4.

strawberry shortcakes

2 x 250g (8 oz) punnets strawberries, hulled and halved
¼ cup caster (superfine) sugar
1 teaspoon vanilla extract
8 store-bought shortbread biscuits
250g (8 oz) mascarpone*
¼ cup (2 fl oz) (single or pouring) cream*
1 tablespoon caster (superfine) sugar, extra

Place the strawberries, sugar and vanilla in a large non-stick frying pan over high heat. Cook for 1–2 minutes or until the sugar has melted and the strawberries have softened slightly. Set aside to cool. Whisk together the mascarpone, cream and extra sugar until smooth. Place half the biscuits in the base of serving bowls or on serving plates. Spoon the mascarpone mixture onto the biscuits and top with the strawberry mixture and remaining biscuits. Serves 4.

Everyone needs a stand-by, done-in-minutes dessert recipe and these strawberry shortcakes are it. If strawberries aren't in season, use sliced figs, nectarines, apricots or soft pears. Otherwise use fresh raspberries.

strawberry shortcakes

style

affogato flavours

Affogato is a shot of espresso coffee poured over a scoop of vanilla ice-cream. For something different, serve it with chocolate, espresso, toffee or caramel ice-cream. Ask your guests which flavour they would prefer, scoop it into a serving glass, serve it with a small glass of espresso and a spoon. Serve affogato instead of or after dessert.

sweet centre

Dessert is made extra-simple and super-quick with these ice-cream filled brioches. Cut circles out of the tops of each brioche and remove some of the middle. Fill the hole with a scoop of your favourite ice-cream and serve immediately. They are an ideal dessert to serve at a cocktail or drinks party. If you can't find brioche, use plain, sweet buns.

ice-cream bar

Make a self-serve ice-cream bar for your guests. Purchase tubs of ice-cream in assorted flavours, then chop up different chocolates and sweets so everyone can add what they like to their favourite ice-cream. Use chocolate-covered honeycomb, malt balls and coconut. You can also put out chocolate fudge sauce and toasted, chopped nuts.

after-dinner mint

For a new take on traditional after-dinner mint chocolates, fill the bottom of each glass with chopped filled or plain chocolate biscuits and top with a scoop of vanilla bean ice-cream. Crush peppermint-flavoured boiled sweets and sprinkle over the top of the ice-cream. As the ice-cream softens your guests will get spoonfuls of all the flavours mixed together.

style

homemade placemats

Draw a plate, knife, fork and glass on paper and use them as disposable placemats to add a unique touch to your table. Use large sheets of paper in any colour you like and draw the shapes in charcoal or crayon to add colour. Go the extra step and write your guests' name above or on the plate if you want everyone to sit in a certain place.

chopstick rest

For a simple but stylish chopstick rest, use a smooth pebble. Put a pebble beside each guest's bowl and place the chopsticks on top. You may also want to lay out Chinese soup spoons if you're serving a noodle soup so your guests can eat the broth. Chopsticks and Chinese soup spoons are inexpensive and available from Asian food stores and supermarkets.

in the news

Use sheets of newspaper from foreign papers as a table runner. They are a great conversation starter, especially if you have invited a group of people who don't all know each other well, and add a focal point to the table. Buy international newpapers from major newsagencies. Start a collection so you can match the paper with the style of food you're serving.

to share

For a quick weeknight get together, place all the cutlery, chopsticks, napkins and glasses in the middle of the table. That way you can get on with the cooking and your guests will have everything they need as the food comes to the table. Buy pairs of disposable chopsticks that come wrapped in paper from Asian food stores.

saturday
night

saturday night

Forget the stresses of the working week and kick back by having a few friends over for dinner. Make a banquet to share or a more traditional three-course dinner. Whatever you choose, cooking is a breeze and the result will be a hit.

ASIAN FUSION

starter thai chicken wonton stack

main chilli-caramelised pork on
cucumber salad

side lemongrass greens

dessert caramelised pineapple tarts

THE CLASSICS

starter white asparagus with taleggio

main bacon-wrapped beef with
red wine glaze

side porcini mash

dessert caramelised crostini with figs

THAI BANQUET

mains shredded duck and chilli noodle salad

crispy fish with chilli ginger glaze
and thai herbs

chicken salad with coconut
milk dressing

dessert melon in lemongrass syrup

ITALIAN FEAST

starter raw tuna, lemon and chilli linguini

main roast garlic baked chicken

side salsa verde potatoes

dessert simple passionfruit soufflés

WINTER FAVOURITES

starter figs with ricotta, prosciutto and
caramelised balsamic

main oregano and preserved lemon
veal cutlets with garlic brown
butter mash

side breadcrumb zucchini

dessert rich chocolate dessert cakes with
raspberry cream

SUMMER SUPPER

starter goat's cheese tarts

main crispy peppered salmon

side fennel and celeriac slaw

dessert coconut plum crumbles

ASIAN FUSION

starter

thai chicken wonton stack

main

chilli-caramelised pork on cucumber salad

side

lemongrass greens

dessert

caramelised pineapple tarts

thai chicken wonton stack

chilli-caramelised pork on cucumber salad

thai chicken wonton stack

vegetable oil for shallow-frying
8 wonton wrappers*
2 cooked chicken breast fillets, shredded
1 cup basil leaves
1 cup mint leaves
1 cup coriander (cilantro) leaves
1 large mild red chilli, seeded and shredded
2 tablespoons lime juice
2 teaspoons fish sauce*
2 teaspoons brown sugar

Heat 1cm (⅓ in) of the oil in a frying pan or wok over high heat. Cook the wonton wrappers in batches until crisp. Drain on absorbent paper. Combine the chicken, basil, mint, coriander and chilli. Place two wontons on each serving plate and top with the chicken mixture. Combine the lime juice, fish sauce and sugar and pour over the wonton stack. Serves 4.

chilli-caramelised pork on cucumber salad

1 tablespoon sesame oil
650g (21 oz) pork fillet, trimmed and sliced
1 tablespoon grated ginger
1 large mild red chilli, seeded and chopped
¼ cup (2 fl oz) soy sauce
⅔ cup brown sugar
1 tablespoon fish sauce*
2 tablespoons lime juice
2 cucumbers, thinly sliced
½ cup bean sprouts
½ cup mint leaves
½ cup coriander (cilantro) leaves

Heat the oil in a large frying pan or wok over high heat. Add the pork and cook for 2 minutes each side or until just cooked through. Remove from the pan and set aside. Reduce the heat to low and add the ginger, chilli, soy sauce, sugar, fish sauce and lime juice to the pan. Stir to dissolve the sugar and then simmer for 8 minutes or until thickened. Add the pork to the pan and toss in the sauce to coat. Combine the cucumber, bean sprouts, mint and coriander and serve with the pork. Serves 4.

lemongrass greens

2 stalks lemongrass*, chopped
½ red onion, chopped
4 kaffir lime leaves*, shredded
1 tablespoon vegetable oil
200g (7 oz) baby bok choy*, trimmed+
200g (7 oz) broccolini*, trimmed
200g (7 oz) gai larn* (chinese broccoli), trimmed
sea salt

Place the lemongrass, onion and lime leaves in a food processor and process until a rough paste forms. Heat the oil in a large frying pan or wok over medium heat. Add the lemongrass paste and cook for 30 seconds or until fragrant. Add the bok choy, broccolini, gai larn and salt and toss to coat. Cover the pan with a lid and cook for 3 minutes or until the greens are tender. Serves 4.
+ Use any combination of crisp green vegetables you have on hand, such as snow peas (mange tout), broccoli, beans, asparagus and sugar snap peas.

caramelised pineapple tarts

250g (8 oz) ready-prepared puff pastry*
2 tablespoons desiccated coconut
8 thin slices pineapple, core removed
40g (1 oz) butter, melted
1 tablespoon brown sugar
coconut ice-cream or sorbet to serve

Preheat the oven to 200°C (390°F). Roll out the pastry on a lightly floured surface until 3mm (⅛ in) thick and cut into 4 x 13cm (5 in) circles. Sprinkle the pastry with the coconut and place two pineapple slices on each circle, leaving a 1cm (⅓ in) border. Brush the pineapple with the butter and sprinkle with the sugar. Place on baking trays lined with non-stick baking paper and bake for 15 minutes or until puffed and golden. Serve with the coconut ice-cream. Serves 4.

lemongrass greens   caramelised pineapple tarts

THE CLASSICS

starter

white asparagus with taleggio

main

bacon-wrapped beef with red wine glaze

side

porcini mash

dessert

caramelised crostini with figs

white asparagus with taleggio

bacon-wrapped beef with red wine glaze + porcini mash

white asparagus with taleggio

400g (14 oz) white asparagus, trimmed and peeled
80g (3 oz) butter
⅓ cup (2½ fl oz) white wine
1½ teaspoons lemon thyme leaves
sea salt and cracked black pepper
4 thick slices taleggio cheese*

Cook the asparagus in a saucepan of boiling water for
2–3 minutes or until just tender. Drain and keep warm.
Place the butter, wine, thyme, salt and pepper in a frying
pan over high heat and cook for 1 minute. Place the
asparagus and taleggio on serving plates and spoon over
the butter sauce. Serves 4.

bacon-wrapped beef with red wine glaze

30g (1 oz) butter
1 leek, sliced
1 tablespoon horseradish
4 x 250g (8 oz) fillet steaks
8 rashers bacon
sea salt and cracked black pepper
red wine glaze
50g (1½ oz) butter, extra
½ cup (4 fl oz) red wine
½ cup (4 fl oz) beef stock*
2 tablespoons red currant jelly*
sea salt and cracked black pepper

Preheat the oven to 180°C (355°F). Heat a frying pan over
high heat. Melt the butter in the pan, add the leek and cook,
stirring, for 3–4 minutes or until softened. Remove from the
heat and stir through the horseradish. For each piece of steak,
lay out two rashers of bacon, overlapping slightly, and top
with the leek. Sprinkle the steaks with the salt and pepper,
wrap in the bacon and secure with kitchen string. Heat a
frying pan over high heat. Cook the steaks for 1–2 minutes
each side. Place on a baking tray lined with non-stick baking
paper and cook for 10–15 minutes or until cooked to your
liking. While the beef is cooking, make the red wine glaze.
Place the extra butter, wine, stock, red currant jelly, salt and
pepper in the pan and boil for 8–10 minutes or until slightly
reduced. Spoon over the red wine glaze and serve with the
porcini mash. Serves 4.

porcini mash

150g (5 oz) mashing potatoes*, peeled and halved
2 tablespoons finely chopped dried porcini mushrooms*
80g (3 oz) butter
½ cup (4 fl oz) milk
sea salt and cracked black pepper

Cook the potatoes and mushrooms in boiling salted water
for 15 minutes or until the potatoes are soft. Drain and
mash with the butter, milk, salt and pepper. Serve with the
bacon-wrapped beef with red wine glaze. Serves 4.

caramelised crostini with figs

60g (2 oz) butter, melted
2 tablespoons icing (confectioner's) sugar
8 large slices of baguette
200g (7 oz) mascarpone*
¼ cup (2 fl oz) milk
2 tablespoons brown sugar
1 teaspoon vanilla extract
4 figs, sliced
brown sugar, extra, for sprinkling

Place the butter and icing sugar in a bowl and mix well to
combine. Brush both sides of the bread with the butter
mixture. Preheat a char-grill pan to medium–high. Toast the
bread on each side until golden brown. Place a slice of bread
on each serving plate. Whisk the mascarpone, milk, brown
sugar and vanilla until thick and smooth. Divide the
mascarpone mixture between the bread slices, top with the
figs and sprinkle with the extra brown sugar. Top with the
remaining bread slices and serve. Serves 4.

Seasonal ingredients that only have a short
availability don't have to ruin a dinner menu.
For the starter, swap the white asparagus for
green asparagus or green beans. Instead of
figs in the dessert, use red apples, firm pears,
peaches, apricots or nectarines.

caramelised crostini with figs

THAI BANQUET

mains

shredded duck and chilli noodle salad

crispy fish with chilli ginger glaze

and thai herbs

chicken salad with coconut milk dressing

dessert

melon in lemongrass syrup

shredded duck and chilli noodle salad

crispy fish with chilli ginger glaze and thai herbs

shredded duck and chilli noodle salad

150g (5 oz) cellophane noodles* (mung bean starch)
4 large mild red chillies, seeded and shredded
4 large mild green chillies, seeded and shredded
1/3 cup chopped roasted peanuts
1½ cups coriander (cilantro) leaves
1½ cups thai basil or basil leaves
1½ cups mint leaves
3 cooked duck breast fillets or 1 cooked chinese
    barbecue duck, shredded
3 tablespoons lime juice
3 tablespoons fish sauce*
2 tablespoons brown sugar

Place the noodles in a bowl and cover with boiling water.
Allow to stand for 2 minutes or until soft. Drain. Toss the
noodles with the red and green chillies, peanuts, coriander,
basil, mint and duck. To serve, combine the lime juice, fish
sauce and brown sugar and pour over the salad. Serves 4.

crispy fish with chilli ginger glaze and thai herbs

4 x 150g (5 oz) firm white fish fillets*, skin on
2 tablespoons rice flour*
vegetable oil for shallow-frying
1 cup coriander (cilantro) leaves
1 cup mint leaves
chilli ginger glaze
¼ cup finely grated ginger
4 large mild red chillies, seeded and shredded
½ cup caster (superfine) sugar
½ cup (4 fl oz) white vinegar
2 teaspoons fish sauce*

To make the chilli ginger glaze, place the ginger, chillies, sugar,
vinegar and fish sauce in a saucepan over medium–high heat
and boil for 3–4 minutes or until slightly thickened. Set aside.
Cut the fish into pieces and toss in the rice flour to coat. Heat
1cm (1/3 in) of the oil in a frying pan over high heat. Cook the
fish in batches, skin-side down, for 3 minutes, turn and cook
for 30 seconds or until cooked through and crisp. Drain on
absorbent paper. Place the fish on serving plates and spoon
over the chilli ginger glaze. Sprinkle with the coriander and
mint and serve. Serves 4.

chicken salad with coconut milk dressing

3 chicken breast fillets, trimmed
¾ cup (6 fl oz) coconut milk
½ teaspoon sea salt
200g (7 oz) baby spinach leaves
6 green onions (scallions), shredded
4 kaffir lime leaves*, very finely shredded
coconut milk dressing
¼ cup (2 fl oz) coconut milk, extra
1 tablespoon lime juice
2 teaspoons fish sauce*
2 teaspoons brown sugar

Place the chicken, coconut milk and salt in a frying pan over
low–medium heat and cook for 12–15 minutes each side or
until cooked through. Remove the chicken from the pan, allow
to cool and slice. Place the spinach, green onions, lime leaves
and chicken on serving plates. To make the coconut milk
dressing, combine the extra coconut milk, lime juice, fish
sauce and sugar. To serve, spoon over the dressing. Serves 4.

melon in lemongrass syrup

2 stalks lemongrass*, quartered
½ cup caster (superfine) sugar
1 cup (8 fl oz) water
¼ honeydew melon*, peeled, seeded and sliced
2 nashi pears*, sliced
store-bought coconut ice-cream or sorbet to serve

Place the lemongrass, sugar and water in a saucepan over
high heat. Bring to the boil and simmer for 3 minutes or
until slightly thickened. Place the melon and pears on serving
plates and spoon over the syrup. Serve with the coconut
ice-cream. Serves 4.

All the dishes on this menu complement each
other. Place the dishes in the middle of the
table to share. That way everyone gets to taste
a bit of everything.

chicken salad with coconut milk dressing   melon in lemongrass syrup

ITALIAN FEAST

starter
raw tuna, lemon and chilli linguini

main
roast garlic baked chicken

side
salsa verde potatoes

dessert
simple passionfruit soufflés

raw tuna, lemon and chilli linguini

roast garlic baked chicken + salsa verde potatoes

raw tuna, lemon and chilli linguini

300g (10 oz) linguini or spaghetti
2 tablespoons olive oil
½ teaspoon dried chilli flakes
2 cloves garlic, crushed
⅓ cup salted capers*, rinsed and dried
⅓ cup (2½ fl oz) lemon juice
sea salt and cracked black pepper
1½ cups shredded rocket (arugula) leaves
150g (5 oz) sashimi tuna*, finely chopped
shaved parmesan cheese to serve

Cook the pasta in a large saucepan of salted boiling water
for 10–12 minutes or until al dente. Drain and keep warm.
Return the pan to the heat, add the oil, chilli flakes, garlic and
capers and cook for 2 minutes. Return the pasta to the pan,
add the lemon juice, salt and pepper and toss to combine.
Divide the pasta between serving plates and top with the
rocket, tuna and parmesan. Serves 4.

roast garlic baked chicken

1 head garlic
1 teaspoon olive oil
80g (3 oz) butter, softened
4 chicken breasts with part wing bone, skin on
sea salt and cracked black pepper

Preheat the oven to 180°C (355°F). Cut the top off the garlic
and drizzle with the oil. Wrap the garlic in foil, place on a
baking tray and bake for 30 minutes or until the garlic is soft.
Allow to cool slightly then squeeze the garlic cloves from the
skin. Combine the garlic and butter. Make a small hole
between the skin and the flesh of the chicken and spoon the
garlic butter under the skin of each chicken breast. Use your
fingers to spread the butter over all the flesh. Sprinkle the
chicken with the salt and pepper. Heat a frying pan over high
heat. Add the chicken, skin-side down, and cook for 2 minutes
or until golden. Turn and cook for 1 minute or until golden.
Place the chicken on a baking tray lined with non-stick baking
paper and bake for 8–10 minutes or until cooked through.
Serve with the salsa verde potatoes. Serves 4.

salsa verde potatoes

12 baby new potatoes, halved
1 tablespoon dijon mustard
2 tablespoons lemon juice
2 cups flat-leaf parsley leaves
1 cup dill leaves
¼ cup (2 fl oz) olive oil
sea salt and cracked black pepper

Steam or boil the potatoes until tender. While the potatoes are
cooking, place the mustard, lemon juice, parsley, dill, oil, salt
and pepper in a food processor and process until finely chopped.
Toss the hot potatoes in the salsa verde and serve with the
roast garlic baked chicken. Serves 4.

simple passionfruit soufflés

melted butter for greasing
caster (superfine) sugar for dusting
150ml (5 fl oz) passionfruit pulp
¼ cup caster (superfine) sugar
2 tablespoons lemon juice
1 tablespoon cornflour (cornstarch)
3 teaspoons water
5 egg whites
⅓ cup caster (superfine) sugar, extra

Preheat the oven to 180°C (355°F). Brush 4 x 1 cup (8 fl oz)
capacity ramekins with the butter, dust with the sugar and
place on a baking tray. Place the passionfruit, sugar and
lemon juice in a small saucepan over low heat and stir until
the sugar is dissolved. Increase the heat and bring to the boil.
Combine the cornflour and water and mix to a smooth paste.
Remove the pan from the heat and whisk in cornflour paste.
Return the pan to the heat and cook, whisking continuously,
for 1 minute. Pour the passionfruit mixture into a large bowl
and refrigerate until cold. Place the egg whites in the bowl of
an electric mixer and beat until soft peaks form. Add the extra
sugar in a thin stream and beat until glossy. Gently fold the
egg white mixture through the passionfruit mixture, spoon into
the ramekins and bake for 12–15 minutes or until risen and
golden. Serve immediately. Serves 4.

simple passionfruit soufflés

WINTER FAVOURITES

starter

figs with ricotta, prosciutto and
caramelised balsamic

main

oregano and preserved lemon
veal cutlets with garlic brown butter mash

side

breadcrumb zucchini

dessert

rich chocolate dessert cakes with
raspberry cream

figs with ricotta, prosciutto and caramelised balsamic

oregano and preserved lemon veal cutlets with garlic brown butter mash

figs with ricotta, prosciutto and caramelised balsamic

4 very thin slices prosciutto*
1 radicchio*, leaves separated
4 figs, halved
150g (5 oz) fresh ricotta cheese
caramelised balsamic
½ cup (4 fl oz) balsamic vinegar*
¼ cup brown sugar

Place the prosciutto under a preheated hot grill (broiler) and cook for 2 minutes or until crisp. Break the prosciutto slices in half. Place the radicchio, figs, ricotta and prosciutto on serving plates. To make the caramelised balsamic, place the vinegar and sugar in a small frying pan over medium heat and cook for 3–4 minutes or until thickened. Cool slightly before spooning over the salad. Serves 4.

oregano and preserved lemon veal cutlets with garlic brown butter mash

2 tablespoons olive oil
¼ cup small sprigs oregano
¼ cup finely sliced preserved lemon rind
4 cloves garlic, sliced
4 veal cutlets
sea salt and cracked black pepper
mashed potatoes to serve
garlic brown butter
60g (2 oz) butter
2 cloves garlic, extra, crushed

Heat a large frying pan over medium heat. Add the oil, oregano, lemon rind and garlic and cook for 2 minutes or until fragrant. Remove the oregano, lemon rind and garlic from the pan leaving the oil. Sprinkle the veal with the salt and pepper and add to the pan. Cook for 3–4 minutes each side or until cooked to your liking. Return the oregano mixture to the pan and toss to coat. To make the garlic brown butter, place the butter in a medium frying pan over medium heat and cook for 1 minute or until browned. Take off the heat and add the garlic. To serve, place the mashed potatoes on serving plates and pour over the garlic brown butter. Top with the veal and spoon over the oregano mixture and pan juices. Serves 4.

breadcrumb zucchini

4 small zucchinis (courgettes), halved lengthwise
80g (3 oz) sliced parmesan cheese
1 cup fresh breadcrumbs
1 tablespoon chopped flat-leaf parsley leaves
sea salt and cracked black pepper
2 tablespoons olive oil

Preheat the oven to 180°C (355°F). Place the zucchini in a single layer in a baking dish and cover with the parmesan. Combine the breadcrumbs, parsley, salt and pepper and sprinkle over the parmesan. Drizzle with the oil and bake for 30 minutes or until golden. Serves 4.

rich chocolate dessert cakes with raspberry cream

100g (3½ oz) dark chocolate, chopped
50g (1½ oz) butter
½ cup brown sugar
½ teaspoon vanilla extract
2 eggs, beaten
⅓ cup plain (all-purpose) flour, sifted
2 tablespoons cocoa powder, sifted
100g (3½ oz) raspberries
½ cup (4 fl oz) thick (double) cream*
cocoa powder, extra, for dusting
raspberries, extra, for serving

Preheat the oven to 180°C (355°F). Place the chocolate and butter in a saucepan over low heat and stir until smooth. Set aside to cool. Add the sugar, vanilla and eggs and mix to combine. Add the flour and cocoa and mix to combine. Pour the mixture into 4 x ½ cup (4 fl oz) capacity non-stick greased muffin tins and bake for 12–15 minutes or until cooked when tested with a skewer. While the cakes are cooking, combine the raspberries and cream. When the cakes are cool, split in half, fill with the raspberry cream and dust with the extra cocoa. Serve with the extra raspberries. Serves 4.

breadcrumb zucchini

rich chocolate dessert cakes with raspberry cream

SUMMER SUPPER

starter

goat's cheese tarts

main

crispy peppered salmon

side

fennel and celeriac slaw

dessert

coconut plum crumbles

goat's cheese tarts

crispy peppered salmon + fennel and celeriac slaw

goat's cheese tarts

500g (1 lb) ready-prepared puff pastry*
150g (5 oz) goat's cheese, sliced
2 tablespoons oregano leaves
sea salt and cracked black pepper
2 tablespoons olive oil
2 cups watercress
balsamic vinegar*
extra virgin olive oil
caramelised onions
1 tablespoon olive oil, extra
1 red onion, sliced
1 tablespoon brown sugar
2 tablespoons balsamic vinegar*, extra
sea salt and cracked black pepper

Preheat the oven to 200°C (390°F). To make the caramelised onions, place the extra oil, onion, sugar, extra vinegar, salt and pepper in a frying pan over medium–high heat. Simmer for 3 minutes or until soft and caramelised. Set aside. Roll out the pastry on a lightly floured surface until 3mm (⅛ in) thick and cut into 8 x 10cm (4 in) circles. Place two pastry circles on top of each other and place on baking trays lined with non-stick baking paper. Spread with the caramelised onions leaving a 1cm (⅓ in) border. Top with the goat's cheese, oregano, salt and pepper. Drizzle with the oil and cook for 15–20 minutes or until puffed and golden. Serve with the watercress tossed in the vinegar and extra virgin olive oil. Serves 4.

crispy peppered salmon

4 x 300g (10 oz) salmon fillets
vegetable oil for brushing
1 tablespoon cracked black pepper
sea salt
1 lemon, cut into eight wedges

Heat a non-stick frying pan over high heat. Brush the salmon with the oil and sprinkle with the pepper and salt on both sides. Cook skin-side down for 4 minutes, turn and cook for a further minute or until cooked to your liking. Place the lemon in the pan and cook for 1 minute each side or until caramelised. Serve with the fennel and celeriac slaw. Serves 4.

fennel and celeriac slaw

500g (1 lb) celeriac* (celery root), peeled and finely sliced
2 x 200g (7 oz) fennel*, trimmed and finely sliced
dressing
½ cup whole-egg mayonnaise
1 tablespoon lemon juice
1 tablespoon horseradish cream
1 tablespoon water

To make the dressing, combine the mayonnaise, lemon juice, horseradish cream and water. Place the celeriac and fennel in a bowl and toss to combine. Pour over the dressing and toss to combine. Serve with the crispy peppered salmon. Serves 4.

coconut plum crumbles

4 large plums, halved and stones removed
¾ cup desiccated coconut
¼ cup caster (superfine) sugar
1 teaspoon vanilla extract
1 egg white
vanilla bean ice-cream to serve

Preheat the oven to 180°C (355°F). Place the plums, cut-side up, in a baking dish. Mix together the coconut, sugar, vanilla and egg white. Fill the plums with the coconut mixture and pile high. Bake for 15 minutes or until golden. Serve warm with the vanilla bean ice-cream. Serves 4.

This is the ideal make-ahead menu. Make the goat's cheese tarts and coconut plum crumbles ahead of time and reheat before serving. The fennel and celeriac slaw can also be made ahead. All that is left to do is cook the salmon.

coconut plum crumbles

style

fortune by name

Fortune cookies make easy, inexpensive and fun placesettings. Write your guests' names on squares of hand-torn paper and slot it into the gap in the cookie. After everyone has taken their seat, they can break open the cookie and read their fortune; it's a great way to get everyone talking at the table. Buy them from Asian food stores or supermarkets.

cheese for one

Make a single-serve cheese platter for each of your guests. That way there is no reaching across the table or waiting for the cheese to be passed to you; everyone can nibble at their leisure. Place a selection of cheeses, a stack of crackers or lavash, and fruit, such as figs and miniature apples, on small bread boards. And don't forget the cheese knives.

antipasto

Antipasto doesn't have to be placed in the middle of the table and shared. Serve dips, olives and prosciutto in small bowls on individual plates with lavash or slices of bread so all your guests have their own portions to eat, and everything you want is right in front of you. Single-serve antipasto is a quick, simple starter for a lunch or dinner.

apple a day

Miniature apples make cute, simple placesettings. Write your guests' names on pieces of paper cut into the shape of a leaf, punch a hole in one end, thread with ribbon and tie it to the apple stem. Place it on printed paper also cut into a leaf shape. You can buy miniature apples from greengrocers. If they are not available, use regular apples or small pears.

style

by candlelight

Give your tealight holders a new lease on life. Using holders of different shapes and sizes, wrap patterned and translucent paper around the outside and secure the paper with velvet and satin ribbons. Place tealight candles inside and light them to make sure the paper is not too close to the flame. And remember, never leave lit candles unattended.

rose cups

Use decorative coffee and tea cups as vases for roses. Cut the stems of the roses quite short and place as many blooms as possible in each cup. Place the cups on a platter or group them in the middle of the table to create a centrepiece. This is a good way to use your favourite cups that are chipped but are too precious to throw away.

liqueur coffee

Let your guests choose what flavour liqueur they would like in their coffee. Decant several different flavoured liqueurs into small carafes and bottles and serve with shots of espresso, milk or cream, and sugar. Everyone can then add the amounts they like. Collect patterned and plain carafes and bottles from antique and junk shops, and garage sales.

edible centrepiece

Stack store-bought meringues, cookies, amaretti or chocolates on plates and use them as a table centrepiece. You can wrap them in coloured tissue or wrapping paper to suit your theme. After dinner your guests can eat them or take them home. During the festive season, place bowls of treats around the house so there is always something for visitors to nibble on.

sunday lunch

sunday lunch

While away the afternoon with good friends and simple, delicious food. Settle in, open a bottle or two of wine and just enjoy each other's company. After all, Sunday is supposed to be the most leisurely day of the week.

INDULGENT AFTERNOON

starter   toasted bread salad

main   roast chicken with caramelised parsnips

side   steamed paper bag greens

dessert   simple lemon puddings

LAZY DAY

starter   tomato and capsicum soup

main   chicken and leek pot pies

side   mint and butter peas

dessert   rhubarb meringue mess

AUTUMN FEAST

starter   pancetta with blue cheese and pear

main   garlic roast lamb cutlets

side   lemon butter pan spinach

dessert   fig pie

ASIAN INSPIRED

starter   simple fish cakes

main   noodles in spicy coconut broth

side   spice-fried pork

dessert   green tea and mint granita

VEGETARIAN FARE

starter   garlic and sage marinated antipasto

main   simple leek and ricotta tarts

side   fennel and parsley salad

dessert   raspberry-spiked chocolate brownies

MEDITERRANEAN MEAL

starter   goat's cheese and sweet capsicum salad

main   schnitzel with black olive crust

side   garlic and tomato simmered beans

dessert   warm apple cinnamon crumb cakes

INDULGENT AFTERNOON

starter

toasted bread salad

main

roast chicken with
caramelised parsnips

side

steamed paper bag greens

dessert

simple lemon puddings

toasted bread salad

roast chicken with caramelised parsnips

toasted bread salad

175g (6 oz) piece crusty sourdough bread
3 tablespoons olive oil
2 cloves garlic, crushed
sea salt and cracked black pepper
70g (2½ oz) mixed salad leaves
4 small fresh mozzarella (bocconcini*) cheeses, torn
3 roma tomatoes, cut into wedges
½ cup flat-leaf parsley leaves
dressing
3 tablespoons red wine vinegar*
2 tablespoons olive oil, extra

Preheat the oven to 180°C (355°F). Tear the bread into bite-size pieces and toss with the oil, garlic, salt and pepper. Place on a baking tray and bake for 15 minutes or until golden and crisp. Set aside to cool. Place the bread, salad leaves, mozzarella, tomatoes and parsley in a serving bowl and toss to combine. To make the dressing, whisk together the vinegar and extra oil, pour over the salad, toss to combine and serve immediately. Serves 4.

roast chicken with caramelised parsnips

4 parsnips, trimmed and peeled
60g (2 oz) butter, melted
sea salt
2 tablespoons brown sugar
2 teaspoons sea salt, extra
2 teaspoons cracked black pepper
2 tablespoons chopped rosemary leaves
4 chicken breast fillets, trimmed
4 slices prosciutto*

Preheat the oven to 200°C (390°F). Cut the parsnips into long strips using a vegetable peeler. Place on a baking tray lined with non-stick baking paper and toss with the butter, salt and sugar. Roast for 10 minutes or until the parsnips are starting to brown. Push the parsnips to one side of the dish. Combine the extra salt, pepper and rosemary and sprinkle over both sides of the chicken. Wrap each chicken breast in a slice of prosciutto and place on the baking tray with the parsnips. Roast for 12 minutes or until the chicken is cooked through. Serve with the parsnips and steamed paper bag greens. Serves 4.

steamed paper bag greens

2 lemons, sliced
150g (5 oz) green beans
12 spears asparagus
1 tablespoon olive oil
sea salt and cracked black pepper

Preheat the oven to 200°C (390°F). Cut 4 x 30cm (12 in) squares of non-stick baking paper. Divide the lemon between the paper squares and top with the beans and asparagus. Drizzle with the oil and sprinkle with the salt and pepper. Fold the paper over the vegetables and fold over the ends to enclose. Place on baking trays and bake for 15 minutes or until the vegetables are just soft. Serves 4.

simple lemon puddings

100g (3½ oz) butter, softened
¾ cup caster (superfine) sugar
2 teaspoons finely grated lemon rind
2 eggs
2 tablespoons lemon juice
½ cup plain (all-purpose) flour
½ teaspoon baking powder
½ cup almond meal (ground almonds)*

Preheat the oven to 170°C (340°F). Place the butter, sugar and lemon rind in the bowl of an electric mixer and beat until light and creamy. Add the eggs and beat well. Add the lemon juice, flour, baking powder and almond meal and mix to combine. Pour mixture into 4 x ¾ cup (6 fl oz) capacity greased ovenproof ramekins and bake for 25–30 minutes or until cooked when tested with a skewer. Serve warm with thick (double) cream and vanilla bean ice-cream. Serves 4.

No time to bake the puddings? Combine 100g (3½ oz) mascarpone, ¼ cup (2 fl oz) cream*, 2 teaspoons sifted icing (confectioner's) sugar and 1 teaspoon finely grated lemon rind and sandwich between shortbread with blueberries.

steamed paper bag greens   simple lemon puddings

LAZY DAY

starter

tomato and capsicum soup

main

chicken and leek pot pies

side

mint and butter peas

dessert

rhubarb meringue mess

tomato and capsicum soup

mint and butter peas + chicken and leek pot pies

tomato and capsicum soup

2 x 400g (14 oz) cans peeled tomatoes
500g (1 lb) store-bought char-grilled
   capsicums (bell peppers)
2 tablespoons olive oil
4 cloves garlic, crushed
2 cups (16 fl oz) chicken stock*
1 tablespoon sugar
sea salt and cracked black pepper
2 tablespoons basil leaves
shaved parmesan cheese to serve

Place the tomatoes and capsicums in a food processor
and process until smooth. Heat the oil and garlic in a
saucepan over medium heat for 1 minute or until fragrant.
Add the tomato mixture, stock, sugar, salt and pepper
and cook for 4–6 minutes or until hot. Top with the basil
and parmesan. Serves 4.

chicken and leek pot pies

1 tablespoon olive oil
2 leeks, sliced
6 chicken thigh fillets, trimmed and chopped
1 tablespoon thyme leaves
2 potatoes, peeled and chopped
1¼ cups (10 fl oz) chicken stock*
½ cup (4 fl oz) (single or pouring) cream*
sea salt and cracked black pepper
300g (10 oz) ready-prepared puff pastry*
1 egg, lightly beaten

Preheat the oven to 200°C (390°F). Heat a large frying
pan over medium heat. Add the oil and leeks and cook for
4 minutes or until soft. Add the chicken, thyme, potatoes
and stock and simmer for 20 minutes or until the chicken
is tender and the potatoes are soft. Stir through the cream,
salt and pepper. Spoon the mixture into 4 x 1½ cup
(12 fl oz) capacity ovenproof dishes. Roll out the pastry
on a lightly floured surface until 3mm (⅛ in) thick. Top the
dishes with the pastry and trim the edges. Brush with the
egg and bake for 15 minutes or until the pastry is puffed
and golden. Serve with the mint and butter peas. Serves 4.

mint and butter peas

3 cups frozen peas
⅔ cup (5 fl oz) chicken stock*
40g (1½ oz) butter
sea salt and cracked black pepper
2 tablespoons chopped mint leaves
2 tablespoons grated parmesan cheese

Place the peas and stock in a saucepan over medium heat
and cook, covered, for 5 minutes or until the peas are soft.
Remove from the heat and roughly mash with the butter,
salt and pepper. Stir through the mint and parmesan and
serve with the chicken and leek pot pies. Serves 4.

rhubarb meringue mess

5 stalks rhubarb, chopped
¾ cup (6 fl oz) orange juice
1 teaspoon vanilla extract
¼ teaspoon ground cinnamon
2 tablespoons caster (superfine) sugar
1 cup (8 fl oz) (single or pouring) cream*
2 tablespoons icing (confectioner's) sugar
4 store-bought meringues

Place the rhubarb, orange juice, vanilla and cinnamon
in a saucepan over medium heat and cook, covered, for
8–10 minutes or until the rhubarb is soft. Stir through the
caster sugar, transfer to a bowl and refrigerate until cold.
Whisk together the cream and icing sugar until thick. To
serve, break the meringues into large pieces and place
in the bottom of serving bowls or glasses. Top with the
rhubarb and cream and serve immediately. Serves 4.

For do-ahead entertaining, make the soup, pies
and rhubarb mixture and freeze. Defrost them in
the fridge before heating. The pies can be heated
from frozen. Place them in a 200°C (390°F)
oven until the pastry is golden, then decrease to
140°C (285°F) so the filling heats through.

rhubarb meringue mess

AUTUMN FEAST

starter

pancetta with blue cheese and pear

main

garlic roast lamb cutlets

side

lemon butter pan spinach

dessert

fig pie

pancetta with blue cheese and pear

garlic roast lamb cutlets

pancetta with blue cheese and pear

8 slices pancetta*
60g (2 oz) rocket (arugula) leaves
1 tablespoon balsamic vinegar*
1 tablespoon olive oil
8 thin slices pear
8 slices blue cheese

Place the pancetta on a baking tray and cook under a hot grill (broiler) for 1–2 minutes or until golden and crisp. Toss the rocket in the vinegar and oil. To serve, place the rocket, pear, blue cheese and pancetta on serving plates. Serves 4.

garlic roast lamb cutlets

12 cloves garlic, peeled
6 x 170g (6 oz) king edward or roasting potatoes, sliced
4 small zucchinis (courgettes), halved lengthwise
1 tablespoon rosemary leaves
2 tablespoons olive oil
sea salt and cracked black pepper
8 double lamb cutlets, trimmed +
mustard mint sauce
1½ cups chopped mint leaves
1½ tablespoons seeded mustard
2½ tablespoons honey

Preheat the oven to 220°C (425°F). Place the garlic, potatoes, zucchinis, rosemary, oil, salt and pepper in a baking dish, toss to combine and roast for 25 minutes. While the vegetables are cooking, heat a frying pan over high heat and brown the lamb on all sides. To make the mustard mint sauce, place the mint, mustard and honey in a bowl and mix to combine. Place the lamb on top of the vegetables. Brush the lamb with some of the mint sauce and roast for a further 8–10 minutes or until the lamb is golden and the potatoes are soft. To serve, place the lamb and vegetables on serving plates and top with the remaining mint sauce. Serve with the lemon butter pan spinach. Serves 4.
+ Your butcher will be able to cut double cutlets for you. They stay moist and tender when roasted. Use only four double cutlets if they are large.

lemon butter pan spinach

60g (2 oz) butter
1 tablespoon finely grated lemon rind
2 cloves garlic, crushed
400g (14 oz) baby spinach leaves
2 tablespoons lemon juice
sea salt and cracked black pepper

Place the butter in a frying pan over high heat. Add the lemon rind and garlic and cook for 1 minute or until the garlic is lightly golden. Add the spinach and turn with tongs until soft and wilted. Pour over the lemon juice and sprinkle with the salt and pepper. Serve immediately with the garlic roast lamb cutlets. Serves 4.

fig pie

280g (10 oz) ready-prepared shortcrust pastry*
½ cup almond meal (ground almonds)*
2 tablespoons plain (all-purpose) flour
¼ cup caster (superfine) sugar
40g (1½ oz) butter, melted
½ teaspoon vanilla extract
2 large figs, sliced +
caster (superfine) sugar, extra, for sprinkling

Preheat the oven to 180°C (355°F). Roll out the pastry on a lightly floured surface until 3mm (⅛ in) thick. Combine the almond meal, flour, sugar, butter and vanilla and spread over the pastry leaving a 3cm (1 in) border. Top with the fig and sprinkle with the extra sugar. Fold the pastry edges to enclose and bake for 25–30 minutes or until the pastry is golden. Serve with thick (double) cream or vanilla bean ice-cream. Serves 4.
+ Depending on the season, replace the figs with peaches, necatrines, apricots, apples or pears.

lemon butter pan spinach   fig pie

ASIAN INSPIRED

starter

simple fish cakes

main

noodles in spicy coconut broth

side

spice-fried pork

dessert

green tea and mint granita

simple fish cakes

noodles in spicy coconut broth + spice-fried pork

simple fish cakes

350g (12⅓ oz) firm white fish fillets*
2 egg whites
2 teaspoons grated ginger
2 tablespoons chopped coriander (cilantro) leaves
3 tablespoons rice flour*
sea salt and cracked black pepper
vegetable oil to shallow fry
lemon wedges to serve
mixed salad leaves to serve

Cut the fish into rough 5mm (¼ in) squares. Place the fish, egg whites, ginger, coriander, rice flour, salt and pepper in a bowl and mix to combine. Heat 1cm (⅓ in) of the oil in a frying pan over medium–high heat. Add heaped tablespoons of the mixture, flatten slightly and cook for 1 minute each side or until lightly golden. Drain on absorbent paper and serve hot with the lemon wedges and salad leaves. Serves 4.

noodles in spicy coconut broth

200g (7 oz) dry rice noodles*
1½ tablespoons red curry paste*
1 stalk lemongrass*, finely chopped
3 kaffir lime leaves*, shredded
2 teaspoons grated ginger
2½ cups (1 pint) coconut milk
1 cup (8 fl oz) chicken stock*
½ cup (4 fl oz) water
200g (7 oz) green beans, trimmed
1 tablespoon fish sauce*
lime wedges to serve

Place the noodles in a bowl, cover with boiling water and stand for 2 minutes or until soft. Drain. Heat a saucepan over high heat. Add the curry paste, lemongrass, lime leaves and ginger and cook for 1 minute or until fragrant. Add the coconut milk, stock and water, bring to the boil and simmer for 3 minutes. Add the beans and cook for a further 3 minutes or until just tender. Stir through the fish sauce. Divide the noodles between serving bowls and pour over the coconut broth. Serve with the lime wedges and top with the spice-fried pork. Serves 4.

spice-fried pork

500g (1 lb) pork fillet, trimmed
1 teaspoon chilli powder
1 teaspoon cracked black pepper
sea salt
1 teaspoon chinese five-spice powder*
1 tablespoon rice flour*
2 tablespoons vegetable oil

Slice the pork into thin rounds. Place in a bowl with the chilli powder, pepper, salt, five-spice powder and rice flour and toss to combine. Heat half the oil in a wok or large frying pan over high heat. Add half the pork and cook for 1 minute each side or until golden. Remove and repeat with the remaining oil and pork. Serve with the noodles in spicy coconut broth. Serves 4.

green tea and mint granita

3 cups (24 fl oz) boiling water
3 quality green tea bags
¾ cup caster (superfine) sugar
⅓ cup (2½ fl oz) lemon juice
1 tablespoon finely chopped mint leaves

Place the water and tea bags in a medium saucepan and stand for 5 minutes for the tea to steep. Remove the tea bags and add the sugar and lemon juice. Place over low heat and stir until the sugar has dissolved. Remove from the heat and cool. Add the mint and pour into a 20 x 30cm (7¾ x 12 in) metal tin and freeze for 1 hour. Rake the top with a fork to break up the ice crystals and return to the freezer. Repeat the process three times or until the granita is snow-like. Serve in small chilled bowls. Serves 4.

Run out of time to make and freeze the granita? Purchase ready-made lemon or lime sorbet and serve scoops in chilled bowls with slices of melon, such as honeydew melon or rockmelon (cantaloupe). Sprinkle with finely chopped fresh mint leaves to serve.

green tea and mint granita

VEGETARIAN FARE

starter

garlic and sage marinated antipasto

main

simple leek and ricotta tarts

side

fennel and parsley salad

dessert

raspberry-spiked chocolate brownies

garlic and sage marinated antipasto

simple leek and ricotta tarts

garlic and sage marinated antipasto

6 artichoke hearts, halved and well drained
200g (7 oz) mixed green and black olives
200g (7 oz) cherry tomatoes, halved
4 tablespoons fruity olive oil
15 sage leaves
3 cloves garlic, sliced
cracked black pepper
2 tablespoons white wine vinegar*
150g (5 oz) fetta cheese, sliced

Combine the artichokes, olives and tomatoes. Place the oil and sage in a small saucepan over medium heat and cook for 1 minute. Add the garlic and pepper and cook for a further 2 minutes or until the sage is crisp. Remove from the heat and stir through the vinegar. Pour over the artichoke mixture and stand for 5 minutes before serving. Serve with the fetta and crispbread biscuits or slices of crusty bread. Serves 4.

simple leek and ricotta tarts

500g (1 lb) fresh ricotta cheese
¼ cup grated parmesan cheese
2 eggs
600g (20 oz) ready-prepared puff pastry*
1 leek, trimmed and finely sliced
45g (1½ oz) butter, melted
2 teaspoons thyme leaves
sea salt and cracked black pepper

Preheat the oven to 180°C (355°F). Place the ricotta, parmesan and eggs in a bowl and whisk until smooth. Roll out the pastry on a lightly floured surface until 3mm (⅛ in) thick. Cut into 4 x 15cm (6 in) squares and place on baking trays lined with non-stick baking paper. Spread the ricotta mixture over the pastry squares leaving a 2cm (¾ in) border. Place the leek on top of the ricotta mixture and brush with the butter. Sprinkle with the thyme, salt and pepper and bake for 25–30 minutes or until the leek is golden. Serve with the fennel and parsley salad. Serves 4.

fennel and parsley salad

4 baby fennel, trimmed and thinly sliced
2 cups flat-leaf parsley leaves
¼ cup (2 fl oz) orange juice
2 tablespoons olive oil
1 tablespoon seeded mustard
sea salt and cracked black pepper

Place the fennel and parsley in a serving bowl and toss to combine. Place the orange juice, oil, mustard, salt and pepper in a bowl and whisk to combine. Pour over the salad and serve with the simple leek and ricotta tarts. Serves 4.

raspberry-spiked chocolate brownies

200g (7 oz) dark chocolate, chopped
250g (8 oz) butter
1¾ cups brown sugar
4 eggs
1⅓ cups plain (all-purpose) flour
¼ teaspoon baking powder
⅓ cup cocoa, sifted
1½ cups raspberries, fresh or frozen +

Preheat the oven to 180°C (355°F). Place the chocolate and butter in a small saucepan over low heat and stir until melted and smooth. Place in a bowl with the sugar and eggs. Sift over the flour, baking powder and cocoa and mix to combine. Pour into a 23cm (9 in) greased square cake tin lined with non-stick baking paper. Top the mixture with the raspberries and bake for 30–35 minutes or until set. Serve warm or cold with thick (double) cream or vanilla bean ice-cream. Makes 16.
+ If using frozen raspberries there is no need to defrost them first. You can also use fresh or frozen blueberries.

fennel and parsley salad

raspberry-spiked chocolate brownies

MEDITERRANEAN MEAL

starter

goat's cheese and sweet capsicum salad

main

schnitzel with black olive crust

side

garlic and tomato simmered beans

dessert

warm apple cinnamon crumb cakes

goat's cheese and sweet capsicum salad

schnitzel with black olive crust with garlic and tomato simmered beans

goat's cheese and sweet capsicum salad

½ cup (4 fl oz) white vinegar
½ cup sugar
½ cup (4 fl oz) water
1 red capsicum (bell pepper), seeded and cut into strips
1 yellow capsicum (bell pepper), seeded and cut into strips
80g (3 oz) rocket (arugula) leaves
150g (5 oz) soft goat's cheese, sliced
2 teaspoons olive oil
sea salt and cracked black pepper

Place the vinegar, sugar and water in a saucepan over medium heat and cook, stirring, for 2 minutes or until the sugar has dissolved. Add the red and yellow capsicum and cook for 5 minutes or until just soft. Drain and reserve liquid. Place the rocket, capsicum and goat's cheese on serving plates. Combine ¼ cup (2 fl oz) of the reserved liquid with the oil, salt and pepper. Pour over the salad and serve. Serves 4.

schnitzel with black olive crust

3 cups fresh breadcrumbs
⅓ cup finely chopped black olives
1 tablespoon chopped oregano leaves
sea salt and cracked black pepper
2 eggs
4 pork, chicken or veal schnitzel steaks
vegetable oil for shallow-frying

Combine the breadcrumbs, olives, oregano, salt and pepper in a large bowl. Place the eggs in a shallow dish and whisk to combine. Dip both sides of each schnitzel in the egg and then press both sides firmly in the breadcrumb mixture. Heat 5mm (¼ in) of the oil in a large frying pan over medium–high heat until hot. Cook the schnitzels two at a time for 2–3 minutes each side or until golden, drain on absorbent paper and keep warm in the oven. Serve with the garlic and tomato simmered beans. Serves 4.

garlic and tomato simmered beans

1 tablespoon olive oil
3 cloves garlic, sliced
4 roma tomatoes, cut into wedges
½ cup (4 fl oz) dry white wine or chicken stock*
300g (10 oz) green or flat beans, trimmed
¼ cup torn basil leaves
sea salt and cracked black pepper

Heat a frying pan over medium heat. Add the oil and garlic and cook for 1 minute or until fragrant. Add the tomatoes and wine and cook for 5 minutes. Add the beans and cook for a further 5 minutes or until just tender. Stir through the basil, salt and pepper and serve with the schnitzel with black olive crust. Serves 4.

warm apple cinnamon crumb cakes

60g (2 oz) butter, softened
⅔ cup caster (superfine) sugar
1 teaspoon ground cinnamon
1 egg
⅓ cup sour cream
1 cup plain (all-purpose) flour
1 teaspoon baking powder
topping
1½ tablespoons plain (all-purpose) flour, extra
1 tablespoon brown sugar
¼ teaspoon ground cinnamon, extra
15g (½ oz) butter, extra, melted
½ green apple, cored and thinly sliced

Preheat the oven to 160°C (320°F). Place the butter, caster sugar, cinnamon, egg, sour cream, flour and baking powder in a food processor and process until smooth. Spoon the mixture into 4 x 1 cup (8 fl oz) capacity greased non-stick muffin tins. To make the topping, combine the extra flour, brown sugar, extra cinnamon and extra butter. Toss the apple in the flour mixture and place on top of the cakes. Sprinkle with any remaining flour mixture. Bake for 25–30 minutes or until the cakes are cooked when tested with a skewer. Serve warm with vanilla bean ice-cream. Serves 4.

warm apple cinnamon crumb cakes

style

time for tea

Fresh mint tea makes a refreshing change from coffee and the usual black teas at the end of a meal. Tie a small bunch of mint together with kitchen string and serve with a glass of boiling water and sugar cubes. Use patterned Moroccan-style glasses or ceramic mugs. Your guests can jiggle the mint in their glass for as little or as long as they like.

buttoned up

Dress up your table with simple homemade napkin rings. Make them using fabric-covered buttons of different sizes in colours to suit your napery. Thread ribbon or elastic through the backs of the buttons, tie to form a loop and slip around rolled or folded napkins. Place one on each plate or stack them at one end of the table if you're entertaining buffet-style.

a touch of glass

Old wine glasses of different heights and shapes make great vases. Group them together for a low, tiered centrepiece. Collect glasses from junk shops and garage sales. Look for ones with etching and scalloped patterns to add extra interest. Glasses are ideal for hibiscus, magnolias, gardenias, camellias and other flowers that don't have very long stems.

take your place

For a more formal meal, make a placesetting for each person using wooden pegs. Place a square of hand-torn, textured cardboard or paper between the teeth of a peg with your guest's name written on it. For extra decoration, put other pegs on the napkin. Buy old and new pegs of different shapes from antique, junk and craft shops, and supermarkets.

style

diy mocha

Instead of cooking dessert, have some fun and serve do-it-yourself mocha. Give everyone a shot of espresso, a bowl of dark chocolate shavings, a cup of steamed milk and a spoon so they can add just the right amounts to suit their taste. To create little curls of chocolate, use a vegetable peeler and shave extra so your guests can nibble while they stir.

flavoured waters

Give plain water a lift by delicately flavouring it. Place slices of green apple and mint leaves, raspberries or lemongrass and pieces of ginger in the water an hour before your guests are due to arrive so it will have just a hint of flavour. Put bottles and carafes filled with the flavoured water and ice along the table so everyone can help themselves.

packed lunch

Pack your guests' lunch in billy cans or pails with lids and head off to the park or beach for a picnic. Line the cans with inexpensive scarves to keep the food secure and place napkins between drink bottles and cutlery to prevent breakages. You can also paint dots or stripes on the outside of the cans so your guests will know which one is theirs.

table runner

For a simple table runner, sew together tea towels. Collect antique tea towels or buy inexpensive ones from kitchen shops and supermarkets. Use all the same pattern or mix and match for a patchwork effect. After you're finished using the runner, soak away the wine stains and throw it in the washing machine. You can also make tablecloths.

special
occasion

special occasion

Cooking for special times doesn't have to be complicated or stressful. Whether it's an intimate dinner for two, a buffet to feed a crowd or an afternoon tea with friends, with these menus any occasion becomes memorable.

DINNER FOR TWO

nibble	seared scallops on crispy wontons
starter	buffalo mozzarella and zucchini salad
main	grilled lobster with pistachio and preserved lemon butter
side	crispy potato cakes
dessert	peaches and raspberries with toasted cream

DINNER PARTY FOR EIGHT

nibble	prawn cocktails
starter	roast tomatoes with goat's cheese croutons
main	pork cutlets with beetroots and onions
dessert	rosewater semifreddo with nougat liqueur mocha

BUFFET FOR TWELVE

starter	salmon carpaccio with campari dressing
main	veal roasted in cherry tomato sauce
sides	baked parmesan risotto
	spinach, green bean and almond salad
dessert	chocolate hazelnut celebration cake

DRINKS PARTY

nibbles	salt and pepper squid
	chilli and lemongrass chicken
	spiced coconut prawns
	sesame pork rice-paper rolls
	prosciutto melts

COCKTAIL PARTY

bites	smoked salmon on herb frittatas
	chicken dumplings with chilli glaze
	rare roast beef with horseradish cream
	carrot and parsnip fritters with marinated fetta
	crispy four cheese puffs

AFTERNOON TEA

nibbles	almond macaroons with chocolate truffle filling
	vanilla bean panna cotta cups with raspberries
	chicken sandwiches
	little apple tarte tatins
	lemon curd cupcakes

DINNER FOR TWO

nibble

seared scallops on crispy wontons

starter

buffalo mozzarella and zucchini salad

main

grilled lobster with pistachio

and preserved lemon butter

side

crispy potato cakes

dessert

peaches and raspberries

with toasted cream

seared scallops on crispy wontons

buffalo mozzarella and zucchini salad

seared scallops on crispy wontons

20g (¾ oz) butter
½ teaspoon finely grated lemon rind
4 scallops, trimmed and cleaned
sea salt and cracked black pepper
1 green onion (scallion), finely sliced
crispy wontons
4 wonton wrappers*
vegetable oil for shallow-frying

To make the crispy wontons, cut a circle from each wonton using a round 5cm (2 in) cookie cutter. Discard the trimmings. Heat 1cm (⅓ in) of the oil in a saucepan over high heat. Cook the wontons two at a time until golden and crisp. Drain on absorbent paper and set aside. Heat a frying pan over high heat. Add the butter and melt. Add the lemon rind and stir. Sprinkle the scallops with the salt and pepper, add to the pan and cook for 20–30 seconds each side or until golden and just cooked through. Place a little of the green onion on each wonton and top with a scallop. Spoon over a little of the pan juices and serve with pre-dinner drinks. Serves 2.

buffalo mozzarella and zucchini salad

1 small green zucchini (courgette), thinly sliced
1 small yellow zucchini (courgette), thinly sliced
3 tablespoons small mint leaves
1½ tablespoons olive oil
1½ tablespoons lemon juice
½ teaspoon caster (superfine) sugar
sea salt and cracked black pepper
1 x 130g (4½ oz) buffalo mozzarella*, halved

Place the zucchinis and mint in a bowl. Combine the oil, lemon juice, sugar, salt and pepper, pour over the salad and toss to combine. Place on serving plates and top with the mozzarella. Serves 2.

grilled lobster with pistachio and preserved lemon butter

2 x 250g (8 oz) raw lobster tails, halved and cleaned
1 lemon, halved
pistachio and preserved lemon butter
80g (3 oz) butter, softened
¼ cup finely chopped raw unsalted pistachio nuts
1½ tablespoons finely chopped preserved lemon rind*
1 tablespoon chopped flat-leaf parsley leaves
sea salt and cracked black pepper

To make the pistachio and preserved lemon butter, place the butter, pistachios, lemon rind, parsley, salt and pepper in a bowl and mix to combine. Spread the butter over the lobster flesh and place on a baking tray. Cook the lobster under a medium preheated grill (broiler) for 8 minutes or until the lobster is cooked through. Serve with the lemon and crispy potato cakes. Serves 2.

Fresh is most definitely best when it comes to seafood. Buy scallops and lobster tails from the fishmonger or fish market as close to the day of serving as possible. At the fishmongers, seafood should be displayed or stored on ice, not in water. The flesh should be white and firm, and have a sweet sea smell. Also, check the lobsters' legs, which shouldn't be discoloured at the joints. If you prefer, use prawns instead of scallops and replace the lobster with firm white fish fillets*.

grilled lobster with pistachio and preserved lemon butter

crispy potato cakes

2 starchy potatoes*, peeled
2 teaspoons rice flour
sea salt
vegetable oil for shallow frying

Cut the potato into long threads using a zester. Place on
absorbent paper and squeeze gently to remove any excess
liquid. Toss the potato in the combined rice flour and salt.
Heat 1cm ($\frac{1}{3}$ in) of the oil in a frying pan over medium–high
heat. Add tablespoonfuls of the potato mixture to the oil,
flatten with a spatula and cook for 3–4 minutes each side or
until golden and crisp. Drain on absorbent paper. Serves 2.

peaches and raspberries with toasted cream

4 egg yolks
$\frac{1}{3}$ cup caster (superfine) sugar
2 tablespoons sweet dessert wine
1 peach, halved
100g (3½ oz) raspberries
1 tablespoon icing (confectioner's) sugar

Preheat the oven to 160°C (320°F). Place the egg yolks,
sugar and wine in a bowl and beat with an electric mixer
for 6–8 minutes or until thick and pale. Divide the peach
and raspberries between two small ovenproof dishes. Pour
over the egg mixture and dust with the icing sugar. Bake
for 12–15 minutes or until golden. Serve warm. Serves 2.

crispy potato cakes   peaches and raspberries with toasted cream

DINNER PARTY FOR EIGHT

nibble

prawn cocktails

starter

roast tomatoes with goat's cheese croutons

main

pork cutlets with beetroots and onions

dessert

rosewater semifreddo with nougat

liqueur mocha

prawn cocktails

roast tomatoes with goat's cheese croutons

prawn cocktails

½ cup whole-egg mayonnaise
2 tablespoons lime juice
1 teaspoon finely grated lime rind
8 baby cos (romaine) lettuce leaves
16 sprigs chervil
16 cooked prawns, peeled
lime wedges to serve

Combine the mayonnaise, lime juice and lime rind. Place the lettuce, chervil and prawns in serving bowls and spoon over the mayonnaise. Serve with the lime. Serves 8.

roast tomatoes with goat's cheese croutons

200g (7 oz) punnet yellow teardrop tomatoes*, halved
250g (8 oz) punnet cherry tomatoes*, halved
250g (8 oz) small tomatoes on the vine*
350g (12 oz) green tomatoes*, halved
3 roma tomatoes*, quartered
⅓ cup oregano leaves
¼ cup (2 fl oz) olive oil
8 slices crusty bread
300g (10 oz) soft goat's cheese
2 tablespoons red wine vinegar*
sea salt and cracked black pepper

Preheat the oven to 180°C (355°F). Place the tomatoes in a baking dish, sprinkle with the oregano and half the oil and cook for 30–40 minutes or until soft. Place the bread under a preheated hot grill (broiler) and toast one side until golden. Spread the untoasted side with the goat's cheese and grill until the cheese is just starting to brown. Place the goat's cheese croutons and tomatoes on serving plates and top with the combined vinegar, salt, pepper and remaining oil. Serves 8.

pork cutlets with beetroots and onions

1½ tablespoons fennel seeds
3 tablespoons roughly chopped sage leaves
3 tablespoons rosemary leaves
½ cup flaked sea salt
8 double pork cutlets, trimmed and scored
8 beetroots, trimmed, cleaned and quartered
24 spring onions, trimmed
¼ cup (2 fl oz) olive oil
2 tablespoons rosemary leaves, extra
2 teaspoons sugar
sea salt and cracked black pepper

Preheat the oven to 220°C (425°F). Place the fennel, sage, rosemary and salt in a small food processor and process to a rough powder. Rub the pork with the fennel mixture and place on a baking tray. In a baking dish, toss the beetroots and spring onions in the combined oil, extra rosemary, sugar, salt and pepper. Place the pork in the oven. After 10 minutes, place the beetroots and spring onions in the oven and roast for a further 20 minutes or until the pork is cooked to your liking. Serves 8.

Crackling is the making of a good pork cutlet. To make sure the crackling goes crisp and crunchy when cooking, ensure that the skin is quite dry. Don't store the pork with the skin of one cutlet resting against the flesh of another or it will absorb the moisture from the meat. The best way to dry out the skin is to leave it uncovered in the fridge for an hour or so.

pork cutlets with beetroots and onions

rosewater semifreddo with nougat

3 eggs
2 egg yolks, extra
1 teaspoon vanilla extract
1 teaspoon rosewater*
1 cup caster (superfine) sugar
1¾ cups (14 fl oz) (single or pouring) cream*
100g (3½ oz) store-bought almond or pistachio nougat,
    sliced or finely chopped

Place the eggs, extra yolks, vanilla, rosewater and sugar in a
heatproof bowl. Place the bowl over a saucepan of simmering
water and whisk for 4–5 minutes or until heated and frothy.
Remove from the heat and beat with an electric mixer for
5–6 minutes or until pale and thick. Place the cream in the
bowl of an electric mixer and beat until very soft peaks form.
Gently fold the egg mixture through the cream until just
combined. Spoon the mixture into 8 x ¾ cup (6 fl oz) capacity
ramekins or freezerproof cups. Cover and freeze for 4–6 hours
or until firm. Serve with the nougat slices on the side or
topped with the chopped nougat. Serves 8.

liqueur mocha

100g (3½ oz) dark chocolate, roughly chopped
½ cup (4 fl oz) (single or pouring) cream*
⅔ cup (5 fl oz) hazelnut liqueur
2 tablespoons icing (confectioner's) sugar
8 shots espresso coffee

Place the chocolate and cream in a small saucepan over
medium heat until melted and smooth. Remove from the
heat, add the hazelnut liqueur and sugar and stir. Pour
into serving glasses and add the coffee. Serves 8.

rosewater semifreddo with nougat   liqueur mocha

BUFFET FOR TWELVE

starter

salmon carpaccio with campari dressing

main

veal roasted in cherry tomato sauce

sides

baked parmesan risotto

spinach, green bean and almond salad

dessert

chocolate hazelnut celebration cake

salmon carpaccio with campari dressing

veal roasted in cherry tomato sauce

baked parmesan risotto

3 cups arborio rice*
8 cups (64 fl oz) chicken stock*
2 cups finely grated parmesan cheese
80g (3 oz) butter
sea salt and cracked black pepper

Preheat the oven to 180°C (355°F). Place the rice and stock in a large baking dish and stir to combine. Cover tightly with foil or a lid and bake for 45 minutes or until most of the stock is absorbed and the rice is al dente. Add the parmesan, butter, salt and pepper and stir for 3–4 minutes or until the risotto is thick and creamy. Serves 12.

spinach, green bean and almond salad

1½ cups slivered almonds
⅓ cup (2½ fl oz) lemon juice
½ cup (4 fl oz) olive oil
⅓ cup (2½ fl oz) chicken stock*
1½ tablespoons dijon mustard
1½ tablespoons finely grated lemon rind
½ teaspoon caster (superfine) sugar
sea salt and cracked black pepper
250g (8 oz) baby spinach leaves
1kg (2 lb) green beans, trimmed and blanched

Toast the almonds in a frying pan over medium heat for 1 minute or until golden. Remove from the pan. Add the lemon juice, oil, stock, mustard, lemon rind, sugar, salt and pepper to the pan and simmer for 1 minute. Place the spinach and beans on a serving plate, top with the almonds, pour over the dressing and serve immediately. Serves 12.

baked parmesan risotto

spinach, green bean and almond salad

salmon carpaccio with campari dressing

2 tablespoons olive oil
½ cup salted capers*, rinsed and dried
1 x 700g (23 oz) sashimi salmon*
120g (4 oz) baby rocket (arugula) leaves
campari dressing
¼ cup (2 fl oz) Campari
¼ cup (2 fl oz) lemon juice
¼ cup (2 fl oz) olive oil, extra
1½ teaspoons sugar
sea salt

Heat a frying pan over medium–high heat. Add the oil and
capers and cook for 2 minutes or until crisp. Set aside. With
a sharp knife very thinly slice the salmon and place on serving
plates. Top with the capers and rocket. To make the Campari
dressing, mix together the Campari, lemon juice, oil, sugar and
salt. Drizzle the Campari dressing over the salmon. Serves 12.

veal roasted in cherry tomato sauce

12 slices provolone cheese*
24 basil leaves
12 veal schnitzel steaks
sea salt and cracked black pepper
olive oil for frying
cherry tomato sauce
3 x 250g (8 oz) punnets cherry tomatoes*, halved
4 cloves garlic, sliced
3 tablespoons oregano leaves
200g (7 oz) black olives
2 tablespoons finely grated lemon rind
3 tablespoons olive oil, extra

Preheat the oven to 180°C (355°F). To make the cherry
tomato sauce, place the tomatoes, garlic, oregano, olives,
lemon rind and extra oil in a large baking dish and toss to
combine. Bake for 40 minutes or until the tomatoes are soft.
Place a slice of provolone and two basil leaves on one half of
each slice of veal and fold to enclose. Sprinkle with the salt
and pepper. Heat a large frying pan over high heat. Add the
oil and cook the veal in batches for 30 seconds each side or
until brown. Place the veal on the tomatoes and spoon over
some of the sauce to coat. Return to the oven and cook for
5 minutes or until the veal is just cooked through. Serves 12.

chocolate hazelnut celebration cake

300g (10 oz) butter, chopped
3 cups brown sugar
4 eggs
1 cup hazelnut meal (ground hazelnuts)* or almond
    meal (ground almonds)*
1 cup (8 fl oz) milk
2 cups plain (all-purpose) flour
2 teaspoons baking powder
1 cup cocoa powder
fresh berries to serve
chocolate icing
1 cup (8 fl oz) (single or pouring) cream*
½ cup cocoa powder, extra, sifted
400g (14 oz) dark chocolate, chopped
150g (5 oz) butter

Preheat the oven to 160°C (320°F). Place the butter and sugar
in the bowl of an electric mixer and beat until light and
creamy. Add the eggs and beat well. Add the hazelnut meal
and milk, sift over the flour, baking powder and cocoa and mix
until combined. Spoon the mixture into 2 x 20cm (8 in) round
greased and lined cake tins and bake for 55 minutes or until
cooked when tested with a skewer. Allow cakes to cool.
To make the chocolate icing, place the cream and extra cocoa
in a saucepan over low heat and stir until smooth. Add the
chocolate and butter and stir until smooth. Place the mixture
in a bowl and refrigerate until cold. Beat the icing with an
electric mixer until light and fluffy. Spread the icing over the
tops of both cakes and place one cake on top of the other.
Keep cool until serving. Serve with the berries. Serves 12.

A filled, double-layer cake is an impressive
dessert to serve, and it's simple too. Make
the cakes up to two days ahead of time and
store them in an airtight container. Spread
the cakes with the icing on the day of serving
so dessert will be ready and waiting even
before anyone arrives.

chocolate hazelnut celebration cake

DRINKS PARTY

nibbles

salt and pepper squid

chilli and lemongrass chicken

spiced coconut prawns

sesame pork rice-paper rolls

prosciutto melts

salt and pepper squid

chilli and lemongrass chicken

salt and pepper squid

1 tablespoon szechwan peppercorns*
½ teaspoon chilli flakes
1½ teaspoons chinese five-spice powder*
2 teaspoons sea salt
½ cup rice flour*
12 small squid hoods, cleaned, quartered and scored
2 egg whites, lightly beaten
vegetable oil for deep frying
lemon wedges to serve

Heat a frying pan over medium heat. Add the peppercorns, chilli flakes, five-spice powder and salt and cook, stirring, for 1 minute or until fragrant. Place the spice mixture in a small food processor and process to a rough powder. Mix half the spice mixture with the rice flour. Dip the squid in the egg whites and toss in the spice mixture to coat. Heat the oil in a large frying pan or wok over high heat. Cook the squid in batches for 1 minute or until crisp. Drain on absorbent paper and toss with the remaining spice mixture. Serve with the lemon. Serves 6–8.

chilli and lemongrass chicken

2 teaspoons sesame oil
2 stalks lemongrass*, very finely chopped
2 large mild red chillies, seeded and chopped
1 tablespoon finely grated ginger
500g (1 lb) chicken mince
3 tablespoons lime juice
3 tablespoons fish sauce*
2 teaspoons brown sugar
¼ cup shredded mint leaves
16 witlof* (belgian endive) or baby cos (romaine) leaves

Heat a frying pan over high heat. Add the oil, lemongrass, chillies and ginger and cook for 1 minute. Add the mince and cook, stirring, for 5 minutes or until the chicken is cooked through. Stir through the lime juice, fish sauce, sugar and mint. Spoon the lemongrass chicken into the witlof and serve. Makes 16.

spiced coconut prawns

1 stalk lemongrass*, very finely chopped
1 tablespoon grated ginger
2 large mild red chillies, finely chopped
2 cloves garlic, crushed
1 tablespoon vegetable oil
3 tablespoons desiccated coconut
1kg (2 lb) green (raw) prawns, peeled and
    cleaned, tails left intact
salt and pepper
lime wedges to serve

Heat a non-stick frying pan over medium heat. Add the lemongrass, ginger, chillies, garlic and oil and cook, stirring, for 2 minutes or until fragrant. Add the coconut and cook for 1 minute or until toasted. Remove from the pan and set aside. Add the prawns, salt and pepper to the pan and cook for 2–3 minutes or until cooked through. Return the coconut spice mixture to the pan and toss with the prawns. Serve warm with the lime. Serves 6–8.

Don't be tied to the kitchen at a drinks party. Have food circulating around at intervals, not continuously, and ask friends to help by passing around the food. Prepare as much as possible before guests arrive so all that is left to do is the assembly and cooking those dishes that need to be served hot. For the salt and pepper squid, clean, quarter and score the squid and store in the fridge. Make the spice mixture in advance, too. The chilli and lemongrass chicken mixture can also be made ahead of time, reheated and spooned into the witlof* (belgian endive) leaves. Also peel and clean the prawns. Make the sesame pork rice-paper rolls and keep them in the fridge, covered with a damp tea towel, so they don't dry out.

spiced coconut prawns

sesame pork rice-paper rolls

1 tablespoon vegetable oil
2 tablespoons sesame seeds
2 tablespoons grated ginger
300g (10 oz) pork fillet, trimmed and sliced
24 rice paper* rounds
½ cup hoisin sauce*
4 cups grated carrot
6 green onions (scallions), sliced
2 cups coriander (cilantro) leaves
2 cups mint leaves
2 cups basil leaves

Heat a frying pan over high heat. Add the oil, sesame seeds
and ginger and cook, stirring, for 2 minutes or until the
sesame seeds are golden. Remove from the pan and set aside.
Add the pork to the pan in batches and cook for 1–2 minutes
or until browned and cooked through. Remove from the heat.
Add to the sesame mixture, mix to combine and set aside.
Soften each round of rice paper in warm water for 1 minute
and pat dry with absorbent paper. To assemble, divide the
pork, hoisin sauce, carrot, green onions, coriander, mint and
basil between the rice papers. Fold over the base and then roll
to enclose the filling. Keep covered with a damp, clean cloth
until ready to serve. Makes 24.

prosciutto melts

12 slices goat's cheese
3 teaspoons thyme leaves
6 slices prosciutto*, halved
12 thick slices baguette
olive oil for brushing

Preheat the oven to 180°C (355°F). Sprinkle the goat's
cheese with the thyme. Wrap a piece of prosciutto around
each slice of the goat's cheese and place on a slice of
baguette. Place on a baking tray and brush with the oil.
Cook for 10–12 minutes or until the goat's cheese has
melted and the baguette is crisp. Makes 12.

Get the drinks party started with an icy mint
cocktail. Place 1½ cups (12 fl oz) cranberry
juice, 10 large scoops ice and ½ cup (4 fl oz)
vodka, gin or campari in a blender and blend
until the ice is well crushed. Add 5 large mint
leaves and blend until the mint is chopped.
Serve in tall glasses with a straw. Make the
drinks in batches as people arrive so the ice
doesn't melt. Serves 4.

sesame pork rice-paper rolls   prosciutto melts

COCKTAIL PARTY

bites

smoked salmon on herb frittatas

chicken dumplings with chilli glaze

rare roast beef with horseradish cream

carrot and parsnip fritters with

marinated fetta

crispy four cheese puffs

smoked salmon on herb frittatas

chicken dumplings with chilli glaze

smoked salmon on herb frittatas

2 eggs, lightly beaten
2 tablespoons (single or pouring) cream*
1 tablespoon finely chopped dill leaves
1 teaspoon finely grated lemon rind
sea salt and cracked black pepper
60g (2 oz) cream cheese, softened
1 tablespoon lemon juice
2 teaspoons salted capers*, rinsed, dried and chopped
4 slices smoked salmon, cut into thirds
¼ red onion, finely sliced

Preheat the oven to 150°C (300°F). Place the eggs, cream, dill, lemon rind, salt and pepper in a bowl and whisk to combine. Pour the egg mixture into 12 x 2 tablespoon capacity greased non-stick mini muffin tins. Cook for 6–8 minutes or until just set. Cool in the tins for 3 minutes before removing. Combine the cream cheese, lemon juice and capers. Top the frittatas with the cream cheese mixture, a piece of smoked salmon and the onion and serve. Makes 12.

chicken dumplings with chilli glaze

300g (10 oz) chicken mince
¼ cup chopped canned water chestnuts*
2 tablespoons chopped coriander (cilantro) leaves
2 teaspoons finely grated ginger
2 tablespoons soy sauce
20 wonton wrappers*
vegetable oil for greasing
chilli glaze
4 large mild red chillies, seeded and sliced
½ cup (4 fl oz) white vinegar
½ cup sugar

Combine the mince, water chestnuts, coriander, ginger and soy sauce. Place tablespoonfuls of the mixture on the wonton wrappers. Brush the edges with water, bring the corners together and press to seal. Place the dumplings in an oiled steamer over a saucepan of boiling water and steam for 8 minutes or until the dumplings are cooked through. To make the chilli glaze, place the chillies, vinegar and sugar in a saucepan over high heat and boil for 8 minutes or until syrupy. To serve, place the dumplings on chinese soup spoons and spoon over the chilli glaze. Makes 20.

rare roast beef with horseradish cream

12 slices baguette
olive oil for brushing
¼ cup sour cream
2 teaspoons horseradish cream
watercress sprigs to serve
250g (8 oz) piece rare roast beef, finely sliced

Brush the bread with a little of the oil and cook on a preheated hot char-grill until golden and crisp on both sides. Combine the sour cream and horseradish cream. To serve, place sprigs of watercress, a slice of beef and a dollop of the sour cream mixture on the bread. Makes 12.

Planning to make lots of different cocktails will only overload the to-do list for a party. Champagne cocktails are simple, so make bellinis, Kir Royales or classic champagne cocktails. For the bellinis, push a ripe, soft peach through a sieve with the back of a wooden spoon and fill a champagne flute a quarter full with the juice. Top with chilled champagne and serve. If peaches aren't in season, use store-bought peach juice. For the Kir Royales, add a dash of crème de cassis to each glass and fill with champagne. To make the classic champagne cocktails, put a few drops of bitters on white sugar cubes and place one in the bottom of each glass. Fill to a quarter full with orange liqueur, then top with champagne and serve. There's no need to buy expensive champagne when making these cocktails (sparkling wine will do), as other flavours will be added to it.

rare roast beef with horseradish cream

carrot and parsnip fritters with marinated fetta

60g (2 oz) rice flour
½ cup (4 fl oz) iced water
2 teaspoons baking powder
1 egg
½ teaspoon ground cumin
1½ cups grated carrot
1½ cups grated parsnip
¼ cup chopped flat-leaf parsley leaves
sea salt and cracked black pepper
¼ cup (2 fl oz) vegetable oil
350g (12⅓ oz) marinated goat's cheese*
wild rocket (arugula) leaves to serve
cracked black pepper to serve

Place the rice flour, water, baking powder, egg, cumin, carrot, parsnip, parsley, salt and pepper in a large bowl and mix to combine. Heat the oil in a large frying pan. Place tablespoons of the carrot mixture in the pan, flatten slightly and cook in batches for 1–2 minutes each side or until golden. Serve warm topped with the goat's cheese, rocket and pepper. Makes 35.

crispy four cheese puffs

½ cup grated cheddar cheese
¼ cup finely grated parmesan cheese
50g (1½ oz) blue cheese, chopped
100g (3½ oz) fresh ricotta cheese
sea salt and cracked black pepper
16 wonton wrappers*
vegetable oil for shallow frying

Combine the cheddar, parmesan, blue cheese, ricotta, salt and pepper. Place 2 tablespoons of the mixture onto each wonton wrapper and wet the edges with a little water. Fold in half and press to seal. Heat 1cm (⅓ in) of the oil in a frying pan over medium–high heat until hot. Fry the wontons in batches until puffed and golden. Drain on absorbent paper. Makes 16.

carrot and parsnip fritters with marinated fetta   crispy four cheese puffs

AFTERNOON TEA

nibbles

almond macaroons with

chocolate truffle filling

vanilla bean panna cotta cups with raspberries

chicken sandwiches

little apple tarte tatins

lemon curd cupcakes

almond macaroons with chocolate truffle filling

vanilla bean panna cotta cups with raspberries

almond macaroons with chocolate truffle filling

⅔ cup blanched almonds
1 cup icing (confectioner's) sugar
2 egg whites
1 tablespoon caster (superfine) sugar
chocolate truffle filling
200g (7 oz) dark chocolate
⅓ cup (2½ fl oz) (single or pouring) cream*

Preheat the oven to 180°C (355°F). Place the almonds and icing sugar in a food processor and process until very finely chopped. Place the egg whites in a bowl and whisk until soft peaks form. Add the caster sugar and beat well. Fold through the almond mixture. Place 2 teaspoonfuls of the mixture on baking trays lined with non-stick baking paper and bake for 8–10 minutes or until crisp on the outside. Allow to cool on the trays. To make the chocolate truffle filling, place the chocolate and cream in a saucepan over low heat and stir until smooth. Refrigerate until thick. Sandwich together the biscuits with a generous spoonful of the chocolate truffle filling. Makes 16.

vanilla bean panna cotta cups with raspberries

¼ cup (2 fl oz) water
3½ teaspoons powdered gelatine
3¼ cups (26 fl oz) (single or pouring) cream*
¾ cup icing (confectioner's) sugar
1 vanilla bean*, split and scraped
1 piece lemon rind
150g (5 oz) raspberries
2 teaspoons icing (confectioner's) sugar, extra

Place the water in a bowl and sprinkle over the gelatine. Set aside for 5 minutes. Place the cream, sugar, vanilla bean and lemon rind in a saucepan over medium–low heat and simmer, stirring occasionally, for 5 minutes. Add the gelatine mixture and stir for 2 minutes. Remove the vanilla bean and lemon rind. Pour into 12 small glasses or cups and refrigerate for 4 hours or until set. To serve, toss the raspberries in the extra icing sugar and place on top of the panna cotta. Makes 12.

chicken sandwiches

12 slices white bread
butter for spreading
2 cups chopped cooked chicken breast fillet
¾ cup whole-egg mayonnaise
2 tablespoons lemon juice
2 tablespoons chopped basil leaves
2 tablespoons shredded mint leaves
sea salt and cracked black pepper
whole-egg mayonnaise, extra, for spreading
⅓ cup finely chopped chives

Spread one side of the bread with the butter. Combine the chicken, mayonnaise, lemon juice, basil, mint, salt and pepper. Divide between half the bread slices and top with remaining bread. Cut into small triangles and brush one side with the extra mayonnaise. Press the mayonnaise into the chives and serve. Makes 24.

Throwing an afternoon tea party is a lot of fun, especially if some of the cooking is done in advance. The lemon curd for the cupcakes will keep in a jar in the fridge for up to two weeks. Bake the macaroons and cupcakes two days ahead of time and after they've cooled, store them in an airtight container. Fill them just before serving. The vanilla bean panna cotta cups can be made two days in advance. Keep them covered in the fridge. The little apple tarte tatins can be made on the morning before the party. Leave them in the tins, then reheat them in the oven just before serving. Make the chicken sandwiches a few hours ahead of time and cover them with a just damp tea towel to stop the bread from drying out.

chicken sandwiches

little apple tarte tatins

butter, melted, for greasing
60g (2 oz) butter, extra
¾ cup caster (superfine) sugar
2 tablespoons water
2 green apples, peeled, cored and sliced
300g (10 oz) ready-prepared puff pastry*

Preheat the oven to 180°C (355°F). Lightly grease 12 x ½ cup (4 fl oz) capacity non-stick muffin tins with the melted butter. Heat a frying pan over medium heat. Add the extra butter and melt. Add the sugar and water and cook, stirring, until the sugar has dissolved. Continue to cook for 5 minutes or until the mixture is a light golden colour. Add the apples and cook for 5 minutes. Arrange the apples in the base of each tin and top with the caramel mixture. Roll out the pastry on a lightly floured surface until 3mm (⅛ in) thick. Cut out rounds of the pastry to fit inside the tins. Bake for 10 minutes or until the pastry is puffed and golden. Allow to stand for 2 minutes then invert onto serving plates. Serve warm or cool with thick (double) cream. Makes 12.

lemon curd cupcakes

125g (4 oz) butter, softened
½ cup caster (superfine) sugar
1 teaspoon vanilla extract
2 eggs
1 cup plain (all-purpose) flour
2 teaspoons baking powder
¼ cup (2 fl oz) milk
icing (confectioner's) sugar for dusting
lemon curd
½ cup (4 fl oz) lemon juice
125g (4 oz) butter, extra, chopped
1 cup caster (superfine) sugar, extra
3 eggs, extra, beaten

Preheat the oven to 180°C (355°F). To make the lemon curd, place the lemon juice, extra butter, extra sugar and extra eggs in a heatproof bowl over a saucepan of rapidly simmering water for 6–8 minutes, stirring continuously, or until the mixture has thickened. Refrigerate until cool. Place the butter, sugar and vanilla in the bowl of an electric mixer and beat until light and creamy. Gradually add the eggs and beat well after each addition. Add the flour, baking powder and milk and beat well. Spoon the mixture into 12 x ½ cup (4 fl oz) capacity muffin tins lined with paper patty cases and bake for 15 minutes or until cooked when tested with a skewer. Set aside to cool. Cut a circle out of each cupcake and fill with the lemon curd. Top with the cupcake circle and dust with the icing sugar. Makes 12.

little apple tarte tatins

lemon curd cupcakes

style

single stem

A single flower in a small juice or nectar bottle is an elegant,
done-in-a-minute table decoration. Use open lisianthus or rose
bloom, remove all the leaves and buds from the stems, and
place in a bottle filled with water. Group the bottles on a plate,
place them in a line down the middle of the table or put one
in front of each guest's plate.

icy treats

An ice-cream and sorbet tasting plate is a simple dessert for
lots of guests. Place eggcups in the freezer to chill, fill them
with different types of ice-cream and sorbet and place on
stacked cake stands. Everyone can pick the flavour they want,
but make sure you scoop enough so there's more than one
for each person. Collect eggcups from antique and junk stores.

stitched up

Give traditional doilies a new lease on life by making them into a table runner. Stitch doilies of different shapes, sizes and colours onto a length of cotton or linen fabric. If you don't have enough to make a runner, make a large placemat to put in the middle of the table. Take care when washing doilies, especially if they are old or family heirlooms, as they can be fragile.

take away

Put together grown-up party favours by filling cellophane bags with store-bought filled macaroons. Make a bag for each guest or couple and tie them up with ribbon. Give them out as guests leave so they can be nibbled on the way home or enjoyed the next day with coffee. You could also use shortbread biscuits, small filled cookies or chocolate truffles.

style

fragrant fruit

Instead of a vase of flowers or a perfumed candle, use fragrant fruit to scent the dining room. Fill a large, decorative bowl with one type of fruit, such as quinces, guavas, persimmons or mangos, and place it on a sideboard or table. They will fill the room with a subtle fragrance that won't clash with food. Choose fruits in season as they will have stronger scent.

cover up

There's no need to have lots of vases of different shapes and sizes to make the perfect floral centrepiece, you can use jars. Place them in white paper sweet bags to hide labels that haven't come off completely or jars that don't match. Start a collection by washing out jam and condiment jars after you've finished eating their contents.

autumn leaves

Bring autumn to the table by using coloured leaves as a table decoration. Cover the table with a white tablecloth, position the leaves on the cloth and top with a piece of sheer fabric. Also put a leaf on each guest's plate. These can be made into quick and easy placesettings by writing each person's name on the leaf with a felt-tip pen.

chocolate block

A delicious and lazy dessert, especially if you're catering for a crowd, is a block of couverture chocolate. Couverture is a bittersweet chocolate high in cocoa butter that goes well with dessert wine, port, muscat or coffee liqueur. After the meal, place the block of chocolate on a platter and let everyone chip away chunks with a small, sharp knife as they sip.

barbecues
+ brunch

barbecues + brunch
Think beyond the usual entertaining times and invite people over for brunch or a mid-afternoon barbecue. They're more laid-back, more relaxed times to get together, so heat up the grill or set the table for brunch.

CLASSIC BBQ
starter	chilli and lime grilled corn
main	steak sandwiches with lemon aioli
side	char-grilled asparagus salad
dessert	peach and passionfruit trifle

SUMMER LUNCH
starter	mushroom and ricotta bruschetta
main	balsamic and lemon chicken
side	summer potato salad
dessert	seared nectarines with caramelised yoghurt

SOUTHERN-STYLE GRILL
starter	chicken, lime and coriander quesadillas
main	crispy fish with green chilli salsa
side	avocado and chickpea salad
dessert	almond wafers with lime sorbet and tequila

SPICED GRILL
starter	grilled eggplant and white bean salad
main	spiced lamb with tahini dressing
side	mint and fetta tabbouli
dessert	date and almond cakes with orange syrup

LATE BREAKFAST
main	three cheese frittata
sides	crispy bacon rosemary ties
	herb-roasted tomatoes
dessert	apple and strawberry galettes

BRUNCH DATE
mains	lemon and sugar puff pancakes
	berry bircher
	raspberry and mango in rosewater syrup
side	almond and maple yoghurt

CLASSIC BBQ

starter

chilli and lime grilled corn

main

steak sandwiches with lemon aioli

side

char-grilled asparagus salad

dessert

peach and passionfruit trifle

chilli and lime grilled corn

steak sandwiches with lemon aioli

chilli and lime grilled corn

80g (3 oz) butter, melted
2 tablespoons finely grated lime rind
½ teaspoon chilli powder
sea salt and cracked black pepper
4 cobs corn, silk removed

Preheat a barbecue or char-grill to medium. Combine the butter, lime rind, chilli powder, salt and pepper. Brush over the corn and cook for 10 minutes turning occasionally and brushing with the butter mixture. Serve topped with any remaining butter mixture. Serves 4.

steak sandwiches with lemon aioli

8 x 100g (3½ oz) sirloin or fillet steaks
sea salt and cracked black pepper
4 slices wood-fired bread, toasted
80g (3 oz) wild rocket (arugula) leaves
lemon aioli
¾ cup whole-egg mayonnaise
2 cloves garlic, crushed
2 tablespoons lemon juice

To make the lemon aioli, combine the mayonnaise, garlic and lemon juice. Preheat a barbecue or char-grill to high. Sprinkle the steak with the salt and pepper and cook for 2 minutes each side or until cooked to your liking. To serve, place the bread on plates and top with the steaks, lemon aioli and rocket. Serves 4.

char-grilled asparagus salad

400g (14 oz) asparagus, trimmed
80g (3 oz) curly endive (frisée)
parmesan cheese shavings to serve
2 tablespoons wholegrain mustard
2 tablespoons honey
2 tablespoons olive oil
sea salt and cracked black pepper

Preheat a barbecue or char-grill to medium. Cook the asparagus for 2 minutes each side or until just tender. Place on a serving plate and top with the endive and parmesan. Whisk together the mustard, honey, oil, salt and pepper, spoon over the salad and serve. Serves 4.

peach and passionfruit trifle

½ cup (4 fl oz) sweet dessert wine
2 tablespoons caster (superfine) sugar
3 passionfruit, pulp only
4 large slices sponge cake* or 8 sponge finger (savoiardi) biscuits*
2 peaches, sliced
¾ cup (6 fl oz) (single or pouring) cream*
1 tablespoon icing (confectioner's) sugar

Place the dessert wine, sugar and passionfruit in a frying pan and simmer for 4 minutes or until slightly thickened. Place the cake on serving plates, top with the peaches and spoon over the dessert wine mixture. Place the cream and sugar in a bowl and whisk until soft peaks form. Serve with the trifle. Serves 4.

char-grilled asparagus salad   peach and passionfruit trifle

SUMMER LUNCH

starter

mushroom and ricotta bruschetta

main

balsamic and lemon chicken

side

summer potato salad

dessert

seared nectarines

with caramelised yoghurt

mushroom and ricotta bruschetta

balsamic and lemon chicken + summer potato salad

mushroom and ricotta bruschetta

4 large slices wood-fired bread
8 small flat (field) mushrooms
olive oil for brushing
1 clove garlic, halved
sea salt and cracked black pepper
100g (3½ oz) fresh ricotta cheese
2 teaspoons thyme leaves
finely grated parmesan cheese to serve
lemon wedges to serve

Preheat a barbecue or char-grill to medium–high. Brush the bread and mushrooms with the oil and cook for 2 minutes each side or until the bread is toasted and the mushrooms are soft. To serve, rub the bread with the garlic and place on serving plates. Top with the mushrooms and sprinkle with the salt, pepper, ricotta, thyme and parmesan. Serve with the lemon wedges. Serves 4.

balsamic and lemon chicken

4 chicken breast fillets, trimmed
4 large sprigs sage
½ cup (4 fl oz) balsamic vinegar*
¼ cup (2 fl oz) lemon juice
2 tablespoons brown sugar
sea salt and cracked black pepper

Place the chicken in a large, shallow dish with the sage. Combine the vinegar, lemon juice, sugar, salt and pepper and pour over the chicken. Refrigerate for 15 minutes to marinate. Preheat a barbecue or char-grill to medium–high. Drain the chicken and sage from the marinade and reserve. Cook the chicken and sage for 4–5 minutes each side or until the chicken is cooked through. While the chicken is cooking, place the marinade in a small saucepan over high heat and cook for 2–3 minutes or until slightly thickened. To serve, slice the chicken into large pieces and place on serving plates with the sage. Spoon over the sauce and serve with the summer potato salad. Serves 4.

summer potato salad

600g (20 oz) kipfler (fingerling) potatoes, sliced
50g (1½ oz) shredded rocket (arugula) leaves
dressing
2 tablespoons chopped preserved lemon rind*
1 tablespoon wholegrain mustard
½ cup whole-egg mayonnaise
2 tablespoons lemon juice
sea salt and cracked black pepper

Place the potatoes in a saucepan of boiling water and cook until tender. Drain and rinse under running water. Toss the potato with the rocket. To make the dressing, place the preserved lemon rind, mustard, mayonnaise, lemon juice, salt and pepper in a bowl and whisk to combine. To serve, pour the dressing over the potatoes and rocket and toss gently. Serve with the balsamic and lemon chicken. Serves 4.

seared nectarines with caramelised yoghurt

½ cup brown sugar
4 nectarines, halved and stones removed
caramelised yoghurt
1½ cups thick natural yoghurt
2 teaspoons vanilla extract
2 tablespoons brown sugar

Place the sugar on a plate and press the cut side of the nectarines into the sugar. Heat a non-stick frying pan over medium–high heat. Place the nectarines in the pan, sugar-side down, and cook for 1 minute or until golden. Remove from the pan. To make the caramelised yoghurt, combine the yoghurt and vanilla. Sprinkle with the sugar and stand for 1 minute so the sugar melts. Serves 4.

seared nectarines with caramelised yoghurt

SOUTHERN-STYLE GRILL

starter

chicken, lime and coriander quesadillas

main

crispy fish with green chilli salsa

side

avocado and chickpea salad

dessert

almond wafers with lime sorbet

and tequila

chicken, lime and coriander quesadillas

crispy fish with green chilli salsa

chicken, lime and coriander quesadillas

2 chicken breast fillets, cooked and thinly sliced
½ tablespoon lime juice
½ cup coriander (cilantro) leaves
1 large mild red chilli, seeded and chopped
2 green onions (scallions), finely sliced
1⅓ cups grated cheddar cheese
sea salt and cracked black pepper
8 small flour or corn tortillas
vegetable oil for brushing
lime wedges to serve
sour cream to serve

Preheat a barbecue or char-grill to medium. Combine the chicken, lime juice, coriander, chilli, green onions, cheddar, salt and pepper. Divide the mixture between half the tortillas and top with the remaining tortillas. Brush both sides with the oil and cook for 2–3 minutes each side or until crisp. Cut in half and serve warm with the lime wedges and sour cream. Serves 4.

crispy fish with green chilli salsa

2 cups coriander (cilantro) leaves
2 tablespoons finely grated lemon rind
2 tablespoons olive oil
sea salt and cracked black pepper
8 x 70g (2½ oz) firm white fish fillets*, skin on
mixed salad leaves to serve
green chilli salsa
5 large mild green chillies
½ red onion, sliced
1 lemon, peeled and chopped
2 teaspoons sugar
sea salt and cracked black pepper

Preheat a barbecue or char-grill to high. To make the green chilli salsa, cook the chillies for 3–4 minutes or until blackened. Halve the chillies, deseed and chop. Combine with the onion, lemon, sugar, salt and pepper. Set aside. Place the coriander, lemon rind, oil, salt and pepper in a food processor and process until smooth. Brush the coriander mixture on the skin of the fish and cook for 3 minutes each side or until cooked through. Place on serving plates, top with the green chilli salsa and serve with the salad leaves. Serves 4.

avocado and chickpea salad

400g (14 oz) can chickpeas (garbanzos), drained and rinsed
1 avocado, peeled and quartered
½ cup mint leaves
4 slices iceberg lettuce
¼ cup (2 fl oz) lime juice
1 tablespoon olive oil
½ teaspoon sugar
sea salt and cracked black pepper

Roughly chop the chickpeas and combine with the avocado and mint. Place the chickpea mixture on the lettuce. Combine the lime juice, oil, sugar, salt and pepper and drizzle over the salad. Serves 4.

almond wafers with lime sorbet and tequila

2 egg whites
½ cup caster (superfine) sugar
¼ cup plain (all-purpose) flour
½ cup almond meal* (ground almonds)
70g (2½ oz) butter, melted and cooled
⅓ cup flaked almonds
store-bought lime sorbet to serve
4 shots tequila, well chilled, to serve
2 passionfruits, halved, to serve

Preheat the oven to 190°C (375°F). Mix the egg whites and sugar. Add the flour, almond meal and butter and mix to combine. Spread the mixture into 4 x 14cm (5½ in) circles on a tray lined with non-stick baking paper. Press the almonds into the mixture and bake for 15 minutes or until golden. Place scoops of lime sorbet in serving bowls, pour the tequila into cold shot glasses and serve with the passionfruit halves and wafers. Makes 4.

On a hot day, salad leaves can wilt. Make sure they stay crisp by refreshing them in iced water. Dry them well and don't dress the leaves until just before serving or they'll lose their crunch.

avocado and chickpea salad

almond wafers with lime sorbet and tequila

SPICED GRILL

starter

grilled eggplant and white bean salad

main

spiced lamb with tahini dressing

side

mint and fetta tabbouli

dessert

date and almond cakes with orange syrup

grilled eggplant and white bean salad

spiced lamb with tahini dressing + mint and fetta tabbouli

grilled eggplant and white bean salad

2 eggplants (aubergines), sliced
4 tablespoons olive oil
sea salt
90g (3 oz) baby spinach leaves
440g (15½ oz) can white beans*, drained and rinsed
250g (8 oz) cherry tomatoes*, sliced
parsley dressing
2 tablespoons sherry vinegar*
1 tablespoon pine nuts
2 cloves garlic, crushed
1½ cups flat-leaf parsley leaves
3 tablespoons olive oil, extra
sea salt and cracked black pepper

Preheat a barbecue or char-grill to hot. Brush the eggplant with the combined oil and salt and cook for 1 minute each side or until soft. To make the parsley dressing, place the vinegar, pine nuts, garlic, parsley, extra oil, salt and pepper in a food processor and process until finely chopped. To serve, arrange the spinach, white beans, tomatoes and eggplant on a serving platter and spoon over the parsley dressing. Serves 4.

spiced lamb with tahini dressing

2 teaspoons ground cumin
½ teaspoon chilli powder
sea salt and cracked black pepper
750g (1⅔ lb) boneless lamb loin, trimmed
flat or turkish bread, toasted, to serve
rocket (arugula) leaves to serve
tahini dressing
½ cup tahini*
⅓ cup (2½ fl oz) water
⅓ cup (2½ fl oz) lemon juice
2 cloves garlic, crushed
1 tablespoon sugar

Combine the cumin, chilli powder, salt and pepper and sprinkle over the lamb. Preheat a barbecue or char-grill to medium–high. Cook the lamb for 4–5 minutes each side or until cooked to your liking. To make the tahini dressing, place the tahini, water, lemon juice, garlic and sugar in a bowl and whisk to combine. To serve, slice the lamb and serve with the tahini dressing, bread, rocket and mint and fetta tabbouli. Serves 4.

mint and fetta tabbouli

1 cup cracked wheat* (burghul/bulghur)
1 cup (8 fl oz) boiling water
1 cup chopped mint leaves
1 cup chopped flat-leaf parsley leaves
6 green onions (scallions), sliced
150g (5 oz) fetta cheese, crumbled
¼ cup (2 fl oz) lemon juice
1 tablespoon olive oil
sea salt and cracked black pepper

Place the wheat and water in a bowl, cover with plastic wrap and stand for 5 minutes or until the water has been absorbed. Mix the wheat with the mint, parsley, green onions, fetta, lemon juice, oil, salt and pepper and toss to combine. Serve with the spiced lamb with tahini dressing. Serves 4.

date and almond cakes with orange syrup

½ cup plain (all-purpose) flour
¾ cup almond meal* (ground almonds)
½ teaspoon baking powder
½ cup caster (superfine) sugar
½ cup roughly chopped pitted dates
75g (2½ oz) butter, melted
2 tablespoons milk
1 egg
orange syrup
½ cup caster (superfine) sugar, extra
½ cup (4 fl oz) orange juice
2 tablespoons finely grated orange rind

Preheat the oven to 160°C (320°F). Place the flour, almond meal, baking powder, sugar and dates in a bowl and mix to combine. Add the butter, milk and egg and mix to combine. Spoon the mixture into greased 1 cup (8 fl oz) capacity muffin tins and bake for 25 minutes or until cooked when tested with a skewer. While the cakes are cooking, make the orange syrup. Place the extra sugar, orange juice and orange rind in a saucepan and stir over low heat until the sugar has dissolved. Simmer for 5–7 minutes or until slightly thickened. Spoon the warm syrup over the warm cakes and serve with thick (double) cream. Serves 4.

date and almond cakes with orange syrup

LATE BREAKFAST

main

three cheese frittata

sides

crispy bacon rosemary ties

herb-roasted tomatoes

dessert

apple and strawberry galettes

crispy bacon rosemary ties

three cheese frittata

crispy bacon rosemary ties

8 rashers smoked bacon, rind removed
8 large sprigs rosemary

Preheat the oven to 180°C (355°F). Wrap each rasher of the bacon around a sprig of rosemary and place in a baking dish. Bake for 20 minutes or until the bacon is crisp. Serve with the three cheese frittata and herb-roasted tomatoes. Serves 4.

three cheese frittata

8 eggs
¾ cup (6 fl oz) milk
sea salt and cracked black pepper
30g (1 oz) butter
¼ cup shredded basil leaves
250g (8 oz) fresh ricotta cheese, drained
1 cup grated aged cheddar cheese
½ cup grated gruyère cheese*
buttered toast to serve

Heat a non-stick frying pan with an ovenproof handle over medium heat. Whisk together the eggs, milk, salt and pepper. Place the butter in the pan and melt. Pour in the egg mixture and sprinkle over the basil, ricotta, cheddar and gruyère. Cook for 3–4 minutes or until the frittata is starting to set around the edges. Place the pan under a preheated hot grill (broiler) and cook for 8–10 minutes or until the frittata is set. Serve warm cut into wedges with the toast, crispy bacon rosemary ties and herb-roasted tomatoes. Serves 4.

herb-roasted tomatoes

4 tomatoes*, halved
24 basil leaves
8 small sprigs thyme
olive oil for drizzling
sea salt and cracked black pepper

Preheat the oven to 180°C (355°F). Cut three slashes in each tomato and push in three basil leaves. Push a sprig of thyme into one slash in each tomato. Place on a baking tray lined with non-stick baking paper, drizzle with the oil and sprinkle with the salt and pepper. Bake for 30 minutes. Serve with the three cheese frittata and crispy bacon rosemary ties. Serves 4.

apple and strawberry galettes

360g (12½ oz) ready-prepared puff pastry*
4 tablespoons strawberry jam (jelly)
¼ cup almond meal* (ground almonds)
1 apple, thinly sliced
100g (3½ oz) strawberries, thinly sliced
1 tablespoon sugar

Preheat the oven to 190°C (375°F). Roll out the pastry on a lightly floured surface to 3mm (⅛ in) thick, cut into 4 x 14cm (5½ in) circles and place on a baking tray lined with non-stick baking paper. Spread each pastry circle with the jam, sprinkle with the almond meal and top with the apple and strawberries. Sprinkle with the sugar and bake for 15–20 minutes or until the pastry is puffed and golden. Serves 4.

herb-roasted tomatoes

apple and strawberry galettes

BRUNCH DATE

mains

lemon and sugar puff pancakes

berry bircher

raspberry and mango in rosewater syrup

side

almond and maple yoghurt

lemon and sugar puff pancakes

berry bircher

lemon and sugar puff pancakes

1 cup plain (all-purpose) flour
2½ teaspoons baking powder
⅓ cup caster (superfine) sugar
200g (7 oz) fresh ricotta cheese
⅔ cup (5 fl oz) milk
2 teaspoons finely grated lemon rind
60g (2 oz) butter, melted
2 eggs, separated
butter, extra, for greasing
1 cup caster (superfine) sugar, extra
lemon wedges to serve

Sift the flour, baking powder and sugar into a bowl. Add the ricotta, milk, lemon rind, butter and egg yolks and mix to combine. In a separate clean bowl, whisk the egg whites until soft peaks form. Fold the egg whites through the flour mixture. Heat a non-stick frying pan over medium–low heat. Add a little of the extra butter to the pan and then add spoonfuls of the mixture and cook for 2–3 minutes each side or until golden and puffed. Remove from the pan and roll in the extra sugar to coat. Repeat with the remaining mixture. Serve with the lemon wedges. Makes 20.

berry bircher

1½ cups rolled oats
1 cup (8 fl oz) apple juice, warmed
½ cup chopped raw unsalted pistachio nuts
½ teaspoon ground cinnamon
1 cup thick natural yoghurt
2 cups mixed berries
maple syrup to serve

Place the oats and apple juice in a bowl, cover with plastic wrap and allow to stand for 30 minutes or until the oats are soft. Mix through the pistachios, cinnamon and yoghurt and half the berries. To serve, top with the remaining berries and maple syrup. Serves 4.

almond and maple yoghurt

½ cup chopped blanched almonds
½ cup (4 fl oz) maple syrup
2 teaspoons vanilla extract
2 cups thick natural yoghurt

Place the almonds in a frying pan over medium heat and stir until golden. Add the maple syrup and vanilla and simmer for 1 minute. Set aside to cool. Divide the yoghurt between four glasses and pour over the almond mixture. Serve with the raspberry and mango in rosewater syrup. Serves 4.

raspberry and mango in rosewater syrup

½ cup sugar
1 cup (8 fl oz) water
½ teaspoon rosewater*
1½ cups raspberries+
2 mangoes, peeled and thickly sliced

Place the sugar and water in a saucepan over low heat and stir until the sugar has dissolved. Simmer for 5 minutes, remove from the heat and stir through the rosewater. Refrigerate until cold. To serve, place the raspberries and mango in a bowl and pour over the rosewater syrup. Serve with the almond and maple yoghurt. Serves 4.
+ Use frozen raspberries and mangoes if fresh aren't available.

Having people over for breakfast or brunch can seem overwhelming. Some of these recipes can be made the day before. Place the bircher in the serving glasses, cover and store in the fridge. Top with the berries and maple syrup just before serving. Make the almond and maple mixture and rosewater syrup and put them both in the fridge until your guests arrive.

raspberry and mango in rosewater syrup + almond and maple yoghurt

style

it's a wrap

To make a glass vase of flowers look especially neat, wrap leaves around the inside to hide the stems. Using banana leaves, wet one side of each leaf so they will stick to the glass, then add the water and flowers. Trim the stems of the flowers before arranging them in the vase so they will last for several days after purchasing.

single serve

Make up individual serves of condiments to match your menu. Buy a small bamboo steamer for each guest from an Asian food store and tie ribbon around the outside. Decant condiments like mayonnaise, tomato sauce and mustard into small jars and bottles, then pack them into the steamers. Place one in front of each guest's plate.

table scent

Instead of flowers, place bunches of herbs in several small jugs along the dining table. Put a combination of different herbs in each jug. Choose varieties that have a strong fragrance, such as mint, thyme, rosemary and basil, or that are included in the dishes you've cooked. After you've finished using them on the table, store them in the fridge for cooking.

you're set

Sushi mats make great placemats. Buy one for each guest and thread ribbon between the gaps in the mat and attach a knife, fork and napkin. You can then roll them up and take them outdoors or on a picnic. Sushi mats are inexpensive and easy to clean – just brush the crumbs out. They are available from Asian food stores and supermarkets.

style

freshen up

After a barbecue pass around a bowl of warm refresher towels so everyone can clean their hands. Fold up a square of muslin or baby face washer for each person and place them in a microwave-proof, lidded bowl. Wet the muslin with water, add a strip of lemon rind and microwave for about 30 seconds. The lemon rind will give the towels a fresh scent.

in bloom

Eggcups make great vases for single blooms. Group them together on a plate with a frangipani, daisy or rose in each one as a centrepiece or put an eggcup in front of every placesetting. To make them into placecards, write the name of each guest on a luggage tag and tie it around the base of each eggcup with kitchen string or ribbon.

iced coffee

On a warm day, skip the hot coffee at brunch and serve iced
coffee the way the Italians do. Just before serving, fill a tall
glass for each person with shaved ice and pour over a shot
of cooled, strong espresso. Top with a dollop of softly
whipped, unsweetend cream. Serve icing (confectioner's)
sugar on the side for those who like it sweet.

centre stage

Use a tealight holder as a floral centrepiece. Take out the
tealight candles, fill the glass holders with water and place
small flowers, such as hydrangeas, inside. For flowers with
longer stems, like lisianthus and miniature roses, place
small glass nectar or juice bottles in the holders. You can
buy tealight holders from junk and antique shops.

glossary

almond meal
Also known as ground almonds, it is available from most supermarkets. Used instead of, or as well as, flour in cakes and desserts. Make your own by processing whole skinned almonds to a fine meal in a food processor or blender (130g/4 oz almonds will give 1 cup almond meal). To remove the skins from almonds, wrap in a tea towel and rub vigorously.

arborio rice
Has a short, plump-looking grain with surface starch which creates a cream with the stock when cooked to al dente in risotto. Substitute with carnaroli rice.

baby bok choy
A mild-flavoured green vegetable, also known as chinese chard or chinese white cabbage. It can be cooked whole after washing. If using the larger type, separate the leaves and trim the white stalks. Limit the cooking time so that it stays green and slightly crisp.

balsamic vinegar
This Italian vinegar, although tart like other varieties, has a less astringent taste and more of a rich, red wine flavour. Like some wines, the older a balsamic vinegar is, the better it tastes.

bocconcini
Fresh mozzarella balls, that are small in size and usually made from cow's milk. Sold in a whey liquid at supermarkets and delicatessens.

broccolini
A cross between gai larn (chinese broccoli) and broccoli, this green vegetable has long, thin stems and small florets. Sold in bunches at supermarkets and greengrocers, it can be substituted for broccoli.

buffalo mozzarella
Made from water buffalo's milk, this is considered to be the best mozzarella. It is sold in whey in balls at specialty food stores and delicatessens.

capers
The small, deep green flower buds of the caper bush. Available packed either in brine or salt. Use salt-packed capers when possible, as the texture is firmer and the flavour superior. Rinse thoroughly before use.

celeriac
A root vegetable (also called celery root) with white flesh and a mild celery flavour. It is available in winter from supermarkets and greengrocers. Use in salads and soups or roast it with meats.

cellophane noodles
See noodles.

cherry tomatoes
See tomatoes.

chinese five-spice powder
This combination of cinnamon, anise pepper, star anise, clove and fennel is excellent with chicken, meats and seafood. It is sold in Asian food stores and most supermarkets.

cracked wheat
Also known as burghul and bulghur, whole wheat is par-boiled, then cracked and dried. It is used in the salad tabbouli. Available from supermarkets.

cream
Pouring or single cream is also called medium cream. It has a butterfat content of 20–30 per cent. Thick or double cream, which is thick enough to be dolloped, has a butterfat content of 45–55 per cent.

fennel
With its mild aniseed flavour and crisp texture, fennel bulbs are ideal for salads or roasted with meats or fish. Available from supermarkets and greengrocers, it is best in spring.

fish sauce
An amber-coloured liquid drained from salted, fermented fish and used in Thai dishes. Available from supermarkets and Asian food stores, where it is often labelled 'nam pla'.

firm white fish fillets
In this book, snapper, barramundi or blue-eye cod fillets have been used where firm white fish fillets are listed in the ingredients. Use any other white fish that has a firm texture, holds it shape when cooked and is quite 'meaty'.

gai larn
A leafy, dark green vegetable, also known as chinese broccoli. Steam, blanch or stir-fry and serve with soy sauce as a simple side dish. Buy from the greengrocers.

green tomatoes
See tomatoes.

gruyère cheese
Originating in Switzerland, this firm cheese is made from cow's milk and is light yellow in colour. Gruyère melts well and is ideal in cooking. Also use it in sandwiches or serve at the end of a meal as part of a cheese plate. Buy from specialty food stores.

haloumi
Firm white Middle Eastern cheese made from sheep's milk. It has a stringy texture and is usually sold in brine. Available from delicatessens and some supermarkets.

hazelnut meal
Available at many supermarkets, it is also called ground hazelnuts. Make your own by processing whole skinned hazelnuts to a fine meal in a food processor or blender (130g/4 oz hazelnuts will give 1 cup hazelnut meal). To remove the skins from hazelnuts, wrap in a tea towel and rub vigorously.

hoisin sauce
A thick, sweet Chinese sauce made from fermented soybeans, sugar, salt and red rice. Used as a dipping sauce or marinade and as the sauce with Peking duck. Available from Asian food stores and most supermarkets.

honeydew melon
A medium-sized melon with yellow skin and green flesh. Buy from supermarkets and greengrocers.

kaffir lime leaves
Fragrant leaves used crushed or shredded in Thai-style dishes. Available fresh or dried in packets from Asian food stores and some greengrocers.

lemongrass
Aromatic grass that is popular in Thai cooking as it gives a spicy, lemony flavour. Sold fresh in Asian food stores and greengrocers.

marinated goat's cheese
Marinated in olive oil, herbs and peppercorns, it is sold in jars at supermarkets and delicatessens.

mascarpone
A fresh Italian triple-cream curd-style cheese. It has a similar consistency to thick (double) cream and is often used in the same way. Available from specialty food stores and many delicatessens and supermarkets.

mashing potatoes
There are so many varieties of potatoes available and some are better for mashing than others. To get creamy, smooth mash use the sebago, pontiac, exton, king edward, nicola or bison. Do not buy if they have a green tinge.

nashi pears
Shaped like an apple but with a pear flavour, this Asian pear has a yellow skin and crisp, white flesh. Buy in summer from greengrocers and supermarkets.

noodles
Like pasta, keep a supply of dried noodles in the pantry for last-minute meals. Fresh noodles will keep in the fridge for a week if you prefer to use those. Available from Asian food stores and most supermarkets.

cellophane noodles
Also called mung bean starch, these noodles are very thin and almost transparent. Soak them in boiling water, drain and add them to other ingredients.

rice noodles
Fine, dry noodles that need to be soaked in boiling water for a short time, then drained, before use.

pancetta
A cured and rolled Italian bacon similiar to prosciutto but softer in texture and less salty. It is sold in slices at delicatessens and can be cooked or eaten raw in antipasto.

porcini mushrooms
Available fresh in the UK and Europe but sold dried in Australia and the US. They have a meaty texture and earthy flavour. Soak them before using and keep the liquid for cooking. Buy from delicatessens and specialty food stores.

preserved lemon rind
Preserved lemons are rubbed with salt, packed in jars, covered with lemon juice and left for about 4 weeks. Remove the flesh and chop the rind for use in cooking. Available from delicatessens and specialty food stores.

prosciutto
Italian ham that has been salted and air-dried for up to 2 years. Paper-thin slices are eaten raw or used to flavour cooked dishes. Also known as parma ham. Substitute with thinly sliced smoked bacon.

provolone cheese
An Italian cheese available from delicatessens and specialty food stores. Made from cow's milk, it has a firm, waxy texture, is pale yellow in colour and has a mild flavour.

puff pastry
This pastry is so time-consuming and quite difficult to make, many cooks choose to use ready-prepared puff pastry. It can be ordered in advance in blocks from patisseries or bought in both block and sheet forms from the supermarket. If buying sheets of puff pastry you may need to layer several to get the desired thickness.

radicchio
A type of chicory that has red leaves and a slightly bitter, peppery flavour. Buy it from the greengrocers and use it in salads. If it isn't available, use rocket or witlof instead.

red currant jelly
This condiment has a slightly tart flavour. It is made from red currants, sugar and lemon juice. Available from specialty food stores and delicatessens, use it to flavour sauces for meat.

red curry paste

Buy good-quality pastes in jars from Asian food stores or the supermarket. When trying a new brand, it is a good idea to add a little at a time to test the heat. Otherwise, make your own.

red curry paste

3 small red chillies
3 cloves garlic, peeled
1 stalk lemongrass*, chopped
4 green onions (scallions), chopped
1 teaspoon shrimp paste*
2 teaspoons brown sugar
3 kaffir lime leaves*, sliced
1 teaspoon finely grated lemon rind
1 teaspoon grated ginger
½ teaspoon tamarind concentrate*
2–3 tablespoons peanut oil

Place all the ingredients except the oil in the bowl of a small food processor or spice grinder. With the motor running, slowly add the oil and process until you have a smooth paste. Refrigerate in an airtight container for up to 2 weeks. Makes ½ cup.

red wine vinegar

Containing red wine, this vinegar is used in salad dressings and sauces for meats. Buy from supermarkets.

rice noodles

See noodles.

rice flour

A fine flour made from ground white rice. Used as a thickening agent, in baking and to coat foods when cooking Asian dishes. Buy from supermarkets.

rice paper

Vietnamese sheets made from rice flour and water, then dried. Dampen them with warm water and use them to make fresh spring rolls. Available from Asian food stores and some supermarkets.

roasting potatoes

For crunchy, golden roast potatoes, use desiree, pontiac, spunta, russet burbank (idaho), sebago. Ensure potatoes do not have any soft spots or a green tinge. They will keep in a cool, dry place for several weeks.

roma tomatoes

See tomatoes.

rosewater

Made from the diluted essence of distilled rose petals, this natural flavouring is traditionally used in Turkish delight as well as puddings, drinks, jellies and syrups. Available from most supermarkets.

salted capers

See capers.

sashimi salmon

Top-grade salmon that can be eaten raw. It is sold with no skin or bones and is available from fishmongers. Buy it as close to serving as possible.

sashimi tuna

Top-grade tuna that can be eaten raw. It is sold with no skin or bones and is available from fishmongers. Buy it as close to serving as possible.

sherry vinegar

The sherry gives this vinegar its mellow, full-bodied flavour. It is ideal for salad dressings and sauces. Available from delicatessens and specialty food stores.

shortcrust pastry

A savoury or sweet pastry that is available ready-made in the frozen section of supermarkets. It is sold in blocks and sheets. Keep a supply for last minute pies and desserts or if you have time, make your own.

shortcrust pastry

2 cups plain (all-purpose) flour
185g (6 oz) cold butter, chopped
2–3 tablespoons iced water

Place the flour and butter in a food processor and process until it resembles fine breadcrumbs. With the motor running, add enough iced water to form a smooth dough and process until just combined. Knead the dough lightly, wrap in plastic wrap and refrigerate for 30 minutes. Preheat the oven to 180°C (355°F). Roll out the pastry on a lightly floured surface or between sheets of non-stick baking paper until 2–3mm (⅛ in) thick and line the tin. Place a piece of non-stick baking paper over the pastry and fill with uncooked rice or beans, or baking weights. Bake for 10 minutes or until the pastry is golden. Add the filling and bake again as the recipe states. Makes 350g (12 oz), which is enough to line a 26cm (10 in) pie dish or tart tin.

sweet shortcrust pastry

2 cups plain (all-purpose) flour
3 tablespoons caster (superfine) sugar
185g (6 oz) cold butter, chopped
2–3 tablespoons iced water

Place the flour, sugar and butter in a food processor and process until it resembles fine breadcrumbs. With the motor running, add enough iced water to form a smooth dough and process until just combined. Knead the dough lightly, wrap in plastic wrap and refrigerate for 30 minutes. Preheat the oven to 180°C (355°F). Roll out the pastry on a lightly floured surface or between sheets of non-stick baking paper until 2–3mm (⅛ in) thick and line the tin. Place a piece of non-stick baking paper over the pastry and fill with uncooked rice or beans, or baking weights. Bake for 10 minutes or until the pastry is golden. Add the filling and bake again as the recipe states. Makes 350g (12 oz), which is enough to line a 26cm (10 in) pie dish or tart tin.

shrimp paste
Also called blachan, this strong-smelling paste is made from salted and fermented dried shrimps pounded with salt. Used in South-East Asian dishes, fry it before using and keep sealed in the fridge. Available from Asian food stores.

star anise
Small, brown seed-cluster that is shaped like a star. It has a strong aniseed flavour that can be used whole or ground in sweet and savoury dishes. Available from supermarkets and specialty food stores.

starchy potatoes
Use starchy potatoes for frying, such as spunta, sebago, russet burbank (idaho), kennebec, colican or patrones.

sponge cake
The basis for many instant desserts, sponge can be bought ready-made from supermarkets or bakeries. You can also make your own.

sponge cake
1¼ cups plain (all-purpose) flour
6 eggs
¾ cup caster (superfine) sugar
60g (2 oz) butter, melted

Preheat the oven to 180°C (355°F). Sift the flour three times. Set aside. Place the eggs and sugar in the bowl of an electric mixer and beat for 8–10 minutes or until thick, pale and tripled in volume. Sift the flour over the egg mixture and gently fold it through. Fold through the butter. Grease two shallow 20cm (8 in) round cake tins or one deep 18cm (7 in) square cake tin. Pour the mixture into the tins and bake for 25 minutes or until the cakes are springy to touch and come away from the sides of the tins. Cool on wire racks. Serves 8–10.

sponge finger biscuits
Sweet, light, finger-shaped Italian biscuits, also known as savoiardi. Great for desserts, such as tiramisu, because they absorb other flavours and soften while maintaining their shape. Available from delicatessens and supermarkets.

stock
Flavoured, strained liquid obtained by simmering bones with vegetables and herbs. Quality stocks are avilable in supermarkets or make your own. Use them in soups, stocks and sauces.

beef stock
1.5kg (3 lb) beef bones, cut into pieces
2 onions, quartered
2 carrots, quartered
2 stalks celery, cut into large pieces
assorted fresh herbs
2 bay leaves
10 peppercorns
4 litres (8 pints) water

Preheat the oven to 220°C (425°F). Place the bones on a baking tray and roast for 30 minutes. Add the onions and carrots and cook for 20 minutes. Transfer the bones, onions and carrots to a stockpot or large saucepan. Add the remaining ingredients. Bring to the boil and simmer for 4–5 hours, skimming regularly. Strain the stock and use, refrigerate for up to 3 days or freeze for up to 3 months. Makes 2½–3 litres (5–6 pints).

chicken stock
1.5kg (3 lb) chicken bones, cut into pieces
2 onions, quartered
2 carrots, quartered
2 stalks celery, cut into large pieces
assorted fresh herbs
2 bay leaves
10 peppercorns
4 litres (8 pints) water

Place all the ingredients in a stockpot or large saucepan. Simmer for 3–4 hours, skimming regularly. Strain and use, refrigerate for up to 3 days or freeze for up to 3 months. Makes 2½–3 litres (5–6 pints).

vegetable stock
4 litres (8 pints) water
1 parsnip
2 onions, quartered
1 clove garlic, peeled
2 carrots, quartered
300g (10 oz) cabbage, roughly chopped
3 stalks celery, cut into large pieces
small bunch mixed fresh herbs
2 bay leaves
1 tablespoon peppercorns

Place all the ingredients in a stockpot or large saucepan and simmer for 2 hours, skimming regularly. Strain and use, or refrigerate for up to 4 days or freeze for up to 8 months. Makes 2½–3 litres (5–6 pints).

szechwan peppercorns
Dried berries with a spicy flavour that are sold whole. Toast in a hot, dry frying pan until fragrant, before crushing or grinding. Available from supermarkets and specialty food stores.

taleggio cheese
This white, washed rind cheese from Italy has a creamy, soft texture and mellow flavour. Made from cow's milk, it can be bought from specialty food stores and delicatessens.

tahini
A thick, smooth, oily paste made from toasted and ground sesame seeds. Available in jars from health food stores and most supermarkets.

tamarind concentrate

Also known as tamarind paste, it is made from the fruit of a tropical tree. It is used in Thai and Indian cooking. Available from Asian food stores and some supermarkets.

teardrop tomatoes

See tomatoes.

tomatoes on the vine

See tomatoes.

tomatoes

At their best in summer and spring, there are many different types of tomatoes. Store them in the fridge but allow them to return to room temperature before eating.

cherry tomatoes

Sweet and bite-sized, they are popular in salads or fried to make a sauce for meats and fish. They are sold in punnets and are deep red or bright yellow in colour.

green tomatoes

There is a variety of tomatoes that are green when ripe but it is fine to use under-ripe regular tomatoes. They have a slightly tart flavour and are ideal for frying and roasting as they hold their shape and don't lose their juices.

roma tomatoes

Also known as egg, plum or Italian tomatoes, these have a mild flavour and firm texture. This is the variety most often sold in cans.

oxheart tomatoes

Large pumpkin-shaped tomatoes, this variety is also called the beefsteak tomato. Ranging in colour from pink and red to black, they can be eaten as is or cooked.

teardrop tomatoes

These small, yellow tomatoes are shaped like tears. They are sold in punnets.

tomatoes on the vine

Small or large tomatoes sold on the vine to give them more flavour and fragrance. They are delicious roasted.

vanilla bean

The pod of an orchid native to Central America. It is added, whole or split, to hot milk or cream to allow the flavour to infuse. Available from specialty food stores, delicatessens and some supermarkets.

vanilla snap biscuits

185g (6 oz) butter
1 cup caster (superfine) sugar
1½ teaspoons vanilla extract
2½ cups plain (all-purpose) flour
1 egg
1 egg yolk, extra

Place the butter, sugar and vanilla in a food processor and process until smooth. Add the flour, egg and extra egg yolk and process until a smooth dough forms. Knead the dough lightly, wrap in plastic and refrigerate for 30 minutes. Preheat the oven to 180°C (355°F). Roll out the dough between two sheets of non-stick baking paper until 5mm (¼ in) thick. Cut the dough into circles using a 5cm (2 in) round cookie cutter. Place on baking trays lined with non-stick paper. Bake for 10–12 minutes or until golden. Cool on wire racks. Makes 45.

vine leaves

Also called grape leaves, as they come from the grape vine, they are used as an edible wrapping for foods, such as cheese. They are an essential ingredient in dolmades/dolmas. They are sold in brine at specialty food stores and delicatessens.

water chestnuts

Available in cans from supermarkets and Asian food stores, these chestnuts are grown in water. They have white flesh and a sweet, nutty flavour and subtle crunch. Chop or slice and use in Asian-style dishes, such as stir-fries and wonton dumplings.

white beans

These small, kidney-shaped beans are also often called cannellini beans. Available from delicatessens and supermarkets either canned or in dried form, which needs to be soaked overnight before using. Use them in salads or to make white bean hummus.

white wine vinegar

Containing white wine, this is more mellow in flavour than regular white vinegar. It is used in salad dressings and sauces or marinades for fish. Buy from supermarkets.

witlof

A slightly bitter salad leaf that can be eaten raw or baked. The tightly packed, small leaves are white with pale green tips. Available from greengrocers and some supermarkets, it is also called belgian endive or chicory.

wonton wrappers

Chinese in origin, these square, thin sheets of dough are avilable fresh or frozen. They can be steamed or fried. Fill them with meat and vegetables to make dumplings for soup or use as a crunchy base for pre-dinner nibbles.

conversion chart

1 teaspoon = 5ml
1 Australian tablespoon = 20ml
  (4 teaspoons)
1 UK & US tablespoon = 15ml
  (3 teaspoons/½ fl oz)
1 cup = 250ml (8 fl oz)

liquid conversions

metric	imperial	US cups
30ml	1 fl oz	⅛ cup
60ml	2 fl oz	¼ cup
80ml	2¾ fl oz	⅓ cup
125ml	4 fl oz	½ cup
185ml	6 fl oz	¾ cup
250ml	8 fl oz	1 cup
375ml	12 fl oz	1½ cups
500ml	16 fl oz	2 cups
600ml	20 fl oz	2½ cups
750ml	24 fl oz	3 cups
1 litre	32 fl oz	4 cups

cup measures

1 cup almond meal (ground almonds)	110g	3½ oz
1 cup breadcrumbs, fresh	50g	2 oz
1 cup sugar, brown	200g	6½ oz
1 cup sugar, white	225g	7 oz
1 cup caster (superfine) sugar	225g	7 oz
1 cup icing (confectioner's) sugar	125g	4 oz
1 cup flour, plain (all-purpose)	125g	4 oz
1 cup rice flour	100g	3½ oz
1 cup rice, cooked	165g	5½ oz
1 cup arborio rice, uncooked	220g	7 oz
1 cup basmati rice, uncooked	220g	7 oz
1 cup couscous, uncooked	180g	6 oz
1 cup lentils, red, uncooked	200g	6½ oz
1 cup polenta, fine, uncooked	180g	6 oz
1 cup basil leaves	45g	1½ oz
1 cup coriander (cilantro) leaves	40g	1¼ oz
1 cup mint leaves	35g	1¼ oz
1 cup flat-leaf parsley leaves	40g	1¼ oz
1 cup cashews, whole	150g	5 oz
1 cup cooked chicken, shredded	150g	5 oz
1 cup olives	175g	6 oz
1 cup parmesan cheese, finely grated	100g	3½ oz
1 cup green peas, frozen	170g	5½ oz

index

donna hay is an Australian-based food stylist, author and magazine editor and one of the best-known names in cookbook and magazine publishing in the world. Her previous eight books have sold more than 2.2 million copies internationally and are renowned for their fresh style, easy-to-follow recipes and inspirational photography. These best-selling, award-winning titles – including *the instant cook, modern classics book* 1 and 2, and *off the shelf* – together with *donna hay magazine,* have captured the imagination of cooks worldwide and set a new benchmark in modern food styling and publishing. She has recently released the extremely popular *donna hay home* range of servingware, kitchenware and foods.